Cambridge E

Elements in Develop.

Series Editor-in-Chief
Kunal Sen
UNU-WIDER and University of Manchester

NEW STRUCTURAL FINANCIAL ECONOMICS

A Framework for Rethinking the Role of Finance in Serving the Real Economy

Justin Yifu Lin
Peking University, Beijing

Jiajun Xu
Peking University, Beijing

Zirong Yang
Chinese Academy of Social Sciences, Beijing

Yilin Zhang
Sun Yat-Sen University, Guangzhou

Shaftesbury Road, Cambridge CB2 8EA, United Kingdom

One Liberty Plaza, 20th Floor, New York, NY 10006, USA

477 Williamstown Road, Port Melbourne, VIC 3207, Australia

314–321, 3rd Floor, Plot 3, Splendor Forum, Jasola District Centre,
New Delhi – 110025, India

103 Penang Road, #05–06/07, Visioncrest Commercial, Singapore 238467

Cambridge University Press is part of Cambridge University Press & Assessment,
a department of the University of Cambridge.

We share the University's mission to contribute to society through the pursuit of
education, learning and research at the highest international levels of excellence.

www.cambridge.org
Information on this title: www.cambridge.org/9781009501712

DOI: 10.1017/9781009501705

© UNU-WIDER 2024

First published 2024

A catalogue record for this publication is available from the British Library.

ISBN 978-1-009-50171-2 Hardback
ISBN 978-1-009-50173-6 Paperback
ISSN 2755-1601 (online)
ISSN 2755-1598 (print)

New Structural Financial Economics

A Framework for Rethinking the Role of Finance in Serving the Real Economy

Elements in Development Economics

DOI: 10.1017/9781009501705
First published online: February 2024

Justin Yifu Lin
Peking University, Beijing

Jiajun Xu
Peking University, Beijing

Zirong Yang
Chinese Academy of Social Sciences, Beijing

Yilin Zhang
Sun Yat-Sen University, Guangzhou

Author for correspondence: Jiajun Xu, jiajunxu@nsd.pku.edu.cn

Abstract: This Element proposes an alternative framework for rethinking the role of finance in serving the real economy from the perspective of new structural financial economics. It challenges the conventional wisdom that developing countries should take the financial structure of developed countries as the benchmark and financial structure does not matter in spurring long-run economic development. As a sub-discipline of new structural economics, new structural financial economics has three tenets. First, examining the appropriate financial structure should take an economy's factor endowment structure as the starting point of analysis, which identifies its latent comparative advantage. Second, the appropriate financial structure is determined by the financing needs of the prevailing production structure. Third, a government should provide development financing to address market failures, and make tailored financial regulations in line with the characteristics of specific financial arrangements. This title is also available as Open Access on Cambridge Core.

This Element also has a video abstract: www.cambridge.org/NSFE_abstract

Keywords: new structural economics, new structural financial economics, factor endowment structure, appropriate financial structure, real economy

ISBNs: 9781009501712 (HB), 9781009501736 (PB), 9781009501705 (OC)
ISSNs: 2755-1601 (online), 2755-1598 (print)

Contents

1 Introduction   1

2 What Is Financial Structure? Does It Matter?   5

3 Determinants of Financial Structures   9

4 Determinants of the Appropriate Financial Structure and Empirical Testing   14

5 The Role of the State in the Financial System   29

6 Why Should Excessive Financialization Be Avoided?   45

7 Conclusion   50

References   52

1 Introduction

In the wake of the global financial crisis that erupted in 2008, financial sector reform has been a key policy focus around the world. The initial focus was primarily on financial stability for preventing a repeat of the financial crisis. Recently, there has been an emerging debate on the broader role of finance in serving the real economy. Acute concerns have been raised on the accelerating process of "financialization" – by which the financial sector has become the dominant master of the broader economy, undercutting its role in serving the real economy (Epstein, 2005). Just as Professor Luigi Zingales, former president of the American Finance Association, argued in his presidential address to the American Finance Association, finance can easily degenerate into a rent-seeking activity without proper rules (Zingales, 2015). He criticized that the financial sector is excessively indulging in speculative activities, undermining its function of serving the financing needs of the real economy.

If the primary role of finance is to serve the real economy, it is important to explore the core question of how finance can better meet the financing needs of the real economy. One prevailing perspective is that developing countries should use the financial structure of developed countries as the benchmark to reform their financial system in an effort to boost long-run economic growth. For instance, Demirgüç-Kunt et al. (2011) construct a variable called "financial structure gap" to measure the deviation of actual financial structure from the estimated optimum, and use countries in the Organisation for Economic Co-operation and Development (OECD) as the benchmark to compute the estimated optimal financial structure. The rationale behind using the financial structure of developed countries as the reference point is that these benchmark countries have "few impediments" to their financial systems (Demirgüç-Kunt et al., 2011: 15). This approach is aligned with that of Rajan and Zingales (1998), which uses the United States as a benchmark for a perfectly functioning financial system. Yet this approach neglects the fact that production structures of developing countries often substantially differ from those of developed countries, and that different industrial sectors have distinct financing needs, which would defy a one-size-fits-all approach. Another prevailing perspective is that it is financial development, rather than financial structure, that matters in determining long-run economic growth. For instance, the World Bank's flagship reports argue that what matters for economic growth is the overall development of the financial system, rather than the relative shares of banks and financial markets. Hence, the World Bank recommends that governments should devote efforts to enhance financial depth and develop enabling legal and regulatory environments instead of optimizing the financial structure (World Bank, 2002,

2013, 2014). Yet this approach fails to realize that different financial arrangements may have distinct comparative advantages in meeting specific financing needs of the real economy. For example, development banks are better positioned to provide long-term finance than are commercial banks (Gong et al., 2023; Hu et al., 2022; Schclarek et al., 2023). Development banks usually do not take household deposits and rely on sovereign creditworthiness to issue long-term bonds on capital markets, which enables development banks to better solve the problem of maturity mismatch.

Centering around how finance better serves the real economy, the present Element proposes the foundation and analytical framework of new structural financial economics (NSFE), which directly engages in the debates on whether developing countries should take the financial structure of developed countries as the benchmark and whether financial structure matters in spurring long-run economic development.[1] NSFE is a subdiscipline of new structural economics (NSE), which reflects the spirit of Marxism's historical materialism and uses the neoclassical approach as its tool for studying the determinants of economic structure and its evolution. From the NSE perspective, an economy consists of a set of interrelated structures, including factor endowment structure (such as labor, capital, and land), production structure (industries and technologies used by each industry), infrastructure (such as irrigation, road, power, and telecommunication), and superstructure (such as financial institution, custom, law, and value), or alternatively, in new institutional economics' terminology, formal and informal institutions. In line with the spirit of historical materialism, NSE maintains that the production structure in an economy is endogenous to the economy's endowments structure, which is given at any specific time and changeable over time. The rationale behind this proposition is that the factor endowment structure determines the economy's latent comparative advantages in industries and technologies used by the industries, that is, the production structure with the lowest possible factor costs of production. To turn comparative advantages in an economy from latent to actual requires adequate infrastructure and superstructure to reduce transaction costs so that the total cost, including production cost and transaction cost,

---

[1] In the classic textbook of finance, finance is defined as "the study of how people allocate scarce resources over time" (Bodie & Merton, 1998: 17). When people implement their decisions, the financial system is an essential "tool" that is defined as "the set of markets and other institutions used for financial contracting and the exchange of assets and risks, and the regulatory bodies that govern all of these institutions." The existing literature on finance mainly focuses on corporate finance and asset pricing. The former deals with decisions regarding a firm's optimal capital structure, which is defined as the mix of debt, equity, and other financing instruments that can maximize the firm's market value, whereas the latter aims to evaluate the market prices for risky assets such as stocks, bonds, and derivatives. Yet, it remains unclear how the financial system can serve the real economy in an effective way.

will be sufficiently low to make the industries competitive in domestic and international markets. This is because different technologies and industries in a production structure have different technical features, such as requirements for specific capital, skill and infrastructure, and economies of scale and risk, and thus require different appropriate infrastructure and superstructure. Otherwise, the lack of appropriate infrastructure and superstructure would result in high transaction costs for the industry's production and its output's trade. Governments can play a facilitating role in removing binding constraints in infrastructure and superstructure to reduce the transaction costs, which would help turn the comparative advantages of technologies and industries in a production structure from latent to actual.[2] Therefore, the appropriate infrastructure and superstructure are endogenous to the production structure and ultimately to the factor endowment structure of the economy (Lin, 2012).

NSFE aims to answer the following three related questions: (1) from the normative perspective, what determines the appropriate financial structure in an economy? (2) from the empirical perspective, what are the determinants of financial structure and its evolution in an economy? and (3) from the policy perspective, what is the adequate role of the state in the determination of the financial system and its evolution and how can it be enhanced? NSFE hopes to make three contributions: First, in line with the main idea of NSE, it emphasizes that the appropriate production structure in an economy at any given time is endogenously determined by the economy's factor endowment structure at that time. Second, it emphasizes that the appropriate financial structure should be endogenously determined according to the financing needs of firms in the prevailing production structure at any given time. Hence, we need to consider the structural differences in factor endowments and production structures between developed countries and developing countries at different development stages to explore the appropriate financial structure that meets divergent financing needs of the real economy in pursuit of high-quality and sustainable development at different stages of development. Third, it emphasizes the synergies between the effective market – which is essential for providing relative factor prices that reflect the relative abundances of factor endowments to guide the entrepreneurs' choices of industries and technologies so that the production structure is in line with the economy's latent comparative advantages determined by the factor endowments – and the facilitating state – which is

---

[2] NSE emphasizes the role of state in mitigating binding constraints to achieve economic structural transformation. This emphasis is in line with the growth diagnostic approach advocated by Hausmann et al. (2005, 2008). What distinguishes NSE from the growth diagnostics approach is that NSE argues that governments should first identify industries with latent comparative advantages before diagnosing specific binding constraints of these industries.

needed for overcoming market failures in the improvement of infrastructure and institutions so as to reduce transaction costs and turn comparative advantages from latent to actual in the economy. Hence, it proposes that a government should tailor its financial policies to improve the financial structure, tailor financial regulation, and adopt pragmatic financial reforms in line with the financing needs of its real economy at different development stages.

The rest of the Element proceeds as follows. In Section 2, we provide working definitions of financial structure and explore whether financial structure matters. From the NSFE perspective, financial structure refers to the relative weights of financial institutions with different features in a financial system. It can be measured from different analytical angles, which depend on the research question at hand. While acknowledging that realizing the functions of financial arrangements requires a supporting environment, as argued by the financial service view (Merton, 1995), NSFE rethinks this mainstream approach by emphasizing that different financial arrangements intrinsically have distinct comparative advantages in meeting divergent financing needs of the real economy. In Section 3, we examine the determinants of financial structures by reflecting on the limitations of the existing explanations and proposing an alternative hypothesis of how the production structure and its change drive the evolution of the financial structure from the NSFE perspective. In Section 4, we propose the analytical framework of NSFE by investigating the distinctive financing demands of the real economy, comparative advantages of different financial arrangements, and the match between divergent financing demands and appropriate financial arrangements, as well as exploring the methods of testing appropriate financial structures. In Section 5, we explore the role of the state in addressing market failures with a special focus on public development financial institutions (PDFIs) in case that commercial financial institutions and private capital markets do not meet the financing needs of the real economy, discuss how governments can make tailored financial regulations in line with the characteristics of specific financial arrangements, and finally examine why governments need to take the pragmatic approach to financial reforms rather than adopting shock therapy. In Section 6, we engage in dialogue with the financialization literature to emphasize that finance should serve the real economy. NSFE echoes the critiques that finance can easily degenerate into a rent-seeking activity and maintains that the principal role of finance is to serve the real economy by financing economic operation and productive investments instead of speculating on short-term returns. We diagnose why finance may be diverted from its principal role and propose how to ensure that finance can serve the real economy. Finally, we conclude with key findings.

2 What Is Financial Structure? Does It Matter?

In this section, we examine what financial structure is, review the existing literature on whether it matters, and justify why it matters from the NSE perspective. The mainstream perspective holds that it is financial development rather than financial structure that matters in deciding long-run economic growth (Levine, 2002). This argument that financial structure does not matter echoes the Modigliani and Miller (MM) theorem, which argues that capital structure is of little relevance in deciding the market value of firms in a perfect and frictionless market. NSFE reflects on the limitations of this conventional wisdom and maintains that financial structure matters because different financial institutions have different comparative advantages in meeting the distinctive demands of the real economy, which has endogenous differences in its production structure at different stages of development.

2.1 A Working Definition of Financial Structure

A structure is defined as the ratio of different components that share common functions while having distinctive features. From the NSFE perspective, the financial structure refers to the relative weights of financial institutions with different features in the financial system. Though different financial institutions may have similar functions such as mobilizing savings, allocating resources, and managing risks, they have distinctive comparative advantages in meeting different demands of the real economy.

The existing literature has been primarily focused on two important aspects of financial structure: the relative importance of financial markets and banks in the financial system, and the distribution of banks of different sizes in the banking industry. Beck and Levine (1999) introduced a new database of indicators of financial development and structure across countries and over time. This database is unique in that it unites a wide variety of indicators that measure the size, activity, and efficiency of financial intermediaries vis-à-vis markets. The existing literature usually uses the proportion of the assets of the top N banks to measure the structure of big banks vis-à-vis small banks (Beck et al., 2004). However, the aforementioned two prevailing measurements of financial structure are not exhaustive.

From the NSFE perspective, financial structure can be measured in alternative ways, which depend on the research question. If we examine the relative merit of capital market versus banks in serving the financing demands of the high-tech industries, we can focus on whether financial activities need to pass through financial intermediaries and measure the financial structure by the ratio of financial markets to financial intermediaries. If we examine whether financial activities are regulated by the government, we can divide financial institutions into formal finance and informal finance. If we examine whether financial institutions are development-oriented or profit-driven, we can measure the financial structure as the relative weight of development banks to commercial banks.

2.2 Does Financial Structure Matter?

The early literature maintains that financial structure matters, and debates which is better – bank-based or market-based financial systems (Allen & Gale, 2000; Diamond, 1984; Holmstrom & Tirole, 1997). The principal-agent theory has often been used to underpin the models in the debates.[3] The bank-based view highlights the positive role of banks in acquiring information about firms and managers and thereby improving capital allocation and corporate governance, managing liquidity risk, and thereby enhancing investment efficiency, mobilizing capital to exploit economies of scale (Allen & Gale, 1999; Diamond, 1984; Siri & Tufano, 1985). The market-based view highlights the growth-enhancing role of well-functioning markets in fostering greater incentives to conduct research, enhancing corporate governance by easing takeovers, and facilitating risk management (Holmstrom & Tirole, 1993; Jensen & Murphy, 1990; Levine, 1991). Since Goldsmith (1969) tried to explore the impact of financial structure upon economic growth, a large number of economists have continued to discuss which is better, bank-based or market-based financial systems, but there is still no consistent conclusion.

Later on, the view that financial structure matters was challenged, as authors of empirical studies failed to find a statistically significant relationship between financial structure and economic performance using a more comprehensive dataset. Allen and Gale (2000) discussed financial systems in five industrial economies and found that the United States and the United Kingdom are market-based financial systems, while Germany, Japan, and France are bank-based financial systems. They noted that all five countries have similar long-run

---

[3] Holmstrom and Tirole (1997) figure that banks and the bond market prevent the moral hazard of enterprises by means of direct monitoring and the self-discipline mechanism respectively. The prerequisite for the self-discipline of enterprises is sufficient collateral (high net asset value). Therefore, under equilibrium conditions, banks and bond markets serve companies with lower and higher net asset value, respectively. In general, enterprises with low net worth are small in scale, while those with high net worth are large in scale. It can be inferred that a bank-dominated financial system is suitable for developing countries dominated by labor-intensive SMEs. In developed countries, the production structure is mostly capital- and technology-intensive with large firm size, and thus capital markets account for a higher proportion of the overall financial system.

growth rates. The experiences of the five countries considered suggest that there is no optimal financial structure and a variety of financial structures can lead to high rates of growth in real per capita GDP.[4] Levine (2002) constructed a broad cross-country dataset to examine market-based and bank-based financial systems. The results indicate that although overall financial development is robustly linked with economic growth, there is no support for either the bank-based or market-based view. Beck and Levine (2002) used cross-country and cross-industry regression analyses and found that having a bank-based or market-based system per se does not seem to greatly affect financing the expansion of industries that depend heavily on external finance, facilitating the formation of new establishments, and improving the efficiency of capital allocation across industries.[5] The view that financial structure does not matter at the macro level echoes the classic theory of the MM theorem that capital structure is of little relevance in deciding the market value of firms at the microlevel. Modigliani and Miller (1958) argued that in a perfect and frictionless financial system, the choice between debt and equity financing has no consequence for the market value of the firm or the cost of capital. The theory assumes that there is no income tax, information asymmetry, or agency cost in the financial market.[6]

---

[4] Yet, from the NSFE perspective, this argument may not hold water. Though all five economies enjoy similar long-run growth rates, they have different production structures and risks of technological progress at their industrialization processes after the Industrial Revolution, and hence need different financial structures. The UK was at the technological frontier after the Industrial Revolution, and the United States quickly caught up with the United Kingdom, whereas Germany, France, and Japan were latecomers and had latecomer advantages in technological progress. After two centuries of development efforts, they have all converged to a global technological frontier similar to that of the United Kingdom and the United States. See further discussion in the first section of Section 3.

[5] Scholars have reflected recently on the mainstream financial structure irrelevance perspective and highlighted that appropriate financial structure may differ at different stages of development, which lends support to the NSFE's argument that financial structure matters. See Cull et al. (2013) for further information.

[6] Many subsequent studies have relaxed the strict hypotheses of perfect markets and reached new insights. The trade-off theory relaxes the assumption that there is no tax and argues that firms seek debt levels that balance the tax advantages of additional debt against the costs of possible financial distress. The pecking order theory argues that information intensity of different financing mechanisms matters and maintains that the firm will borrow, rather than issuing equity, when internal cash flow is not sufficient to fund capital expenditures. The free cash flow theory emphasizes that the agency cost matters and argues that because managers may use their discretion of allocating a firm's operating cash flow to maximize their personal interests rather than maximizing the shareholder's value, dangerously high debt levels will increase value, albeit under the threat of financial distress, when significantly exceeding the profitable investment opportunities (Myers, 2001). The ownership structure theory developed by Jensen and Meckling (1976) relaxes the assumption that there is no agency cost and argues that there exists the optimal combination of debt and equity for a given scale of firms, and this solution is Pareto optimal, in other words, there is no way to reduce agency cost without making someone worse off.

The prevailing view that financial structure does not matter is reinforced by the financial service view, which stresses that financial arrangements – contracts, markets, and intermediaries – arise to ameliorate market imperfections and provide financial services (Levine, 1997; Merton & Bodie, 2006). The financial services view argues that what matters is how the financial arrangements assess potential investment opportunities, exert corporate control, facilitate risk management, enhance liquidity, and ease savings mobilization. In short, the main issue is not banks versus markets. Instead, it is important to have different financial systems to provide efficient financial services to facilitate economic growth. Accordingly, the financial services view highlights how to create better-functioning banks or markets and relegates the bank-based versus market-based debate to the background.

An influential strand of the financial-services view is the law and finance view (La Porta et al., 1997, 1998). The law and finance view argues that finance is a set of contracts defined by legal rights and enforcement mechanisms. A good legal system can increase the confidence of investors and make them believe that investment can obtain reliable returns. As for whether investors invest through banks or stock markets, the channel itself is not important. This view has been supported by the empirical regression analysis that legal system efficiency boosts industry growth, new establishment formation, and efficient capital allocation (Beck & Levine, 2002).

2.3 Why Financial Structure Matters from the NSFE Perspective

While acknowledging that realizing the functions of financial arrangements requires a supporting environment, NSFE rethinks this mainstream approach by emphasizing that different financial arrangements intrinsically have distinct comparative advantages in meeting divergent financing needs of different industrial structures with different capital requirements and risk profiles for their operations and investments in the real economy. It also states that the structure of the real economy differs at different stages of development, causing the appropriate financial structure to be different accordingly.

One possible reason why the recent cross-country regression analysis has not identified a statistically significant association between financial structure and economic performance is that there is no optimal financial structure suitable for all countries. For instance, Boyd and Smith (1998) argue that banks are particularly important at low levels of economic development. Demirgüç-Kunt et al. (2013) empirically find that securities markets become more important as economies develop. Tadesse (2002) examined the relation between the financial structure and economic performance in the real sector. This author found that whereas market-based systems outperform bank-based systems among countries with developed financial sectors, bank-based systems fare better among countries with underdeveloped financial sectors. The preceding findings suggest that there is no one-size-fits-all optimal financial structure that can be applied across countries at different stages of economic development. From the NSFE perspective, while it is acknowledged that realizing the function of financial arrangements needs an enabling institutional environment, it maintains that the appropriate financial structure of economies at different stages of development hinges on distinctive and evolving financing needs of underlying production structures.

One strategic underlying assumption behind the MM theorem is that firms can be divided into "equivalent return" classes such that the return on the shares issued by any firm in any given class is proportional to (and hence perfectly correlated with) the return on the shares issued by any other firm in the same class (Modigliani & Miller, 1958: 266). This assumption neglects the substantial variation in the industrial structure to which firms belong and thus the capital requirement, size, and sources of risk of firms. The empirical evidence shows that firms from different industries have distinctive capital structures. For instance, large, integrated oil companies from technologically mature industries have relied mostly on debt for external financing, whereas the major pharmaceutical companies with huge technological risks typically operate at negative debt ratios (Myers, 2001). Although authors of the existing studies have explored how firm characteristics may affect capital structures, it is worth investigating the extent to which firm characteristics may be influenced by production structures where firms are embedded. Hence, it is promising to explore how industrial characteristics may affect the appropriate capital structure for firms.

In summary, NSFE argues that financial structure matters when examining how finance can best service the real economy, which has different production structures at different stages of development. NSFE maintains that different financial arrangements have their own advantages and disadvantages in mobilizing savings, dispersing risks, and allocating funds. NSFE is not defying the role of institutions in realizing the functions of financial arrangements, but it emphasizes that certain functions are not perfectly substitutable across different financial arrangements.

3 Determinants of Financial Structures

In this section, we first document the variation in financial structures across countries and over time, evaluate the merits and limitations of the existing explanations of what accounts for such variations, and arrive at alternative explanations from the NSFE perspective.

3.1 Variation in Financial Structures

There are substantial variations in the financial structure across countries and over time. Taking the financial structure measured by the relative weight of financial markets to banks as an example, Lin et al. (2013) showed the evolution of financial structure across income groups and over time and identified the following stylized facts: first, the cross-country data shows that the more developed the economy, the higher the share of the stock market in the financial structure; second, the time-series data reveals that the share of the stock market in the financial structure tends to gain more weight as economies move to a more advanced stage of development. The history of the financial structure of the United Kingdom and the United States confirms that large banks and stock markets are playing an increasingly important role in the financial system as economies grow. During the English Industrial Revolution, industrial enterprises were typically extremely small. Interestingly, the English banks were also typically small and locally based with a limited number of offices until at least the mid-nineteenth century. The bank merger movement in England did not arise until the 1860s; it was not until 1918 that the "Big Five" banks came to dominate the English banking system. The London capital market, despite its current prominent role in the national and international financial system, did not make any significant direct contribution to capital formation in the English Industrial Revolution. It was not until the end of the nineteenth century that the capital market started to play an important role in financing industrial sectors. In the United States, before 1890, industrial firms were numerous, small, and closely owned by a limited number of shareholders. As late as the end of the nineteenth century, it was still rare for manufacturing or other non-infrastructural firms to be listed on exchanges. In fact, there was no large-scale market in common stocks prior to 1920. A variety of local financial institutions emerged to meet the needs of small and medium-sized firms in the economy (Lin et al., 2013).

Furthermore, there are variations in financial structure among countries even within the same income group. Figure 1 shows substantial differences in the financial structure among the United Kingdom, the United States, Germany, and Japan. The financial structure of the United Kingdom and the United States was more dominated by the stock market, whereas the financial structure of Germany and Japan was more dominated by banks before 2000. Nevertheless, the financial structures in these four advanced countries converge to a similar profile after 2000.

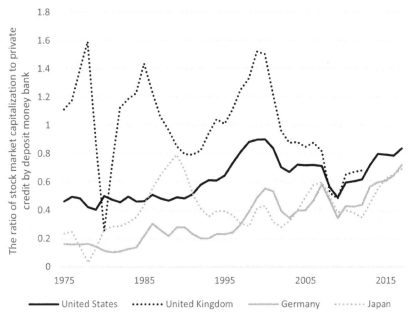

Figure 1 Financial structure in major developed economies
Data source: World Bank, Global Financial Development Database.

3.2 The Existing Explanations of Variation in Financial Structures

To explain why the financial structure of Germany and Japan was bank-based whereas that of the United Kingdom and the United States was market-based, one existing explanation argues that legal origin matters – civil law countries have much weaker investor protection than common law countries, resulting in less developed capital markets (La Porta et al., 1997). Using a sample of forty-nine countries, La Porta et al. (1997) found that weak investor protection in civil law countries, as measured by both the possibility of legal rules in protecting investors and a survey-based estimate of the quality of law enforcement, is associated with the underdevelopment of capital markets.

However, the "legal origin" theory cannot explain the puzzle of why the ratio of France's stock market capitalization to GDP was twice as high as that of the United States in 1913 (Rajan & Zingales, 2003) and why the financial strucure in the mjaor developed countries have been converging after 2000 as shown in Figure 1. If this theory holds water, we would expect that the stock market in France was much less developed than the US stock market. Furthermore, the "legal origin" theory is of little use in explaining changes in financial structure over time, given that the legal origin is a time-invariant variable. For instance, despite their current prominent role in the national financial system, capital markets did not start to play an important role in financing industrial sectors in the United Kingdom until the end of the nineteenth century (Collins, 1988). In fact, the financial structure of the United Kingdom was bank-based during the Industrial Revolution: because industrial enterprises were typically extremely small, the English banks had been small and locally based until at least the mid-nineteenth century (Cameron, 1992; Cameron et al., 1967). This bank-based pattern has also been applied to the early history of the US financial system (Cull et al., 2006).

Another strand of theory holds that culture matters in explaining variations in the financial structure. Stulz and Williamson (2003) argued that differences in cultures, proxied by differences in religion and language, cannot be ignored when examining why investor protection differs across countries. After controlling for the legal origin, they found that civil law Protestant countries have stronger creditor rights than civil law Catholic countries. Hence, they concluded that although legal origin matters in explaining variations in shareholder rights, culture plays a key role in explaining the variation in creditor right protection. Hence, they infer that Catholic countries may have less developed debt markets.[7] Similar to the legal origin theory, the culture theory maintains that the protection of investor rights, including both shareholder rights and creditor rights, is crucial for fostering certain types of financial arrangements.

Yet, the culture theory may be of little help in explaining changes in financial structure over time because culture, such as the principal region or language, is relatively stable. Another major limitation is that both the legal origin theory and the culture theory assume that a particular form of legal or cultural tradition is necessary for enforcing financial agreements. Consequently, they may neglect viable alternative institutional arrangements that can perform the same function (Lin 1989). For instance, Miao et al. (2021) documented that a large bank loan market – the trusted assistant loan market in nineteenth-century China – emerged even in the absence of contracting institutions. They argued that the repayment of trusted assistants was enforced through expertise leverage, which was sufficiently strong to implement enforceable financial agreements and support a large lending market.

A third strand of literature argues that history matters. Monnet and Quintin (2007) presented a dynamic, general equilibrium model in which past fundamentals of an economy (including the cost of bank intermediation, the cost of entry on the financial market, and the distribution of project characteristics) justify a unique, efficient path for its financial system. For instance, they argued that the reason why the United States is a market-based financial system

---

[7] In a similar vein, Kwok and Tadesse (2006) argued that countries characterized by higher uncertainty avoidance are more likely to have a bank-based financial system.

whereas Germany is a bank-based one is that federal laws discouraged bank intermediation in the United States while Germany used to impose significant legal barriers to entry into financial markets. Therefore, despite the convergence in the legal framework, the financial structure in the United States and Germany continues to vary markedly. Although path dependency may play a role in the development of financial institutions, it still begs the question of why governments foster certain types of financial arrangement while depressing others at the initial phase and why they all converged to a similar financial structure once they reached the same advanced development stage.

3.3 The NSFE Perspective

From the NSE perspective, production structure, namely the combination of different industries and different technologies used in each industry, determines the financing demand and firm's risk profile of the real economy. Production structure in an economy is endogenous to the economy's factor endowments structure because the factor endowments structure determines the economy's comparative advantages and thus the appropriate technologies and industries; the endowments structure is given at any specific time and changeable over time, and correspondingly, the production structure of the economy varies (Lin, 2012). From the NSFE perspective, a key determinant of financial structure is production structure because the role of finance is to serve the real economy's operation and investment. If we define the financial structure as the relative weight of banks versus capital markets, NSFE would predict that high-income countries are likely to develop full-fledged capital markets to meet the financing needs of the industrial structure that is at the global technological frontier and relies on costly and risky R&D for technological innovation and industrial upgrading. The rationale is that banks are more appropriate for the financing of traditional asset-intensive industries, whereas capital markets favor innovative and risky projects. Allen et al. (2018) deployed a panel dataset of 108 countries over the sample period 1972–2015 to test whether countries with predominant tangible-asset-intensive industries are more likely to exhibit a bank-based financial system. Furthermore, they used a difference-in-difference strategy to conduct event studies by exploring how the financial structure responds to shocks to the industrial structure. They found that the stock markets experienced significantly faster growth than the banking system after the service sector gained more importance. From this perspective, the variation in the financial structure between the United States and Germany lies in the divergence in their industrial structure. Financial systems in countries such as Germany would remain bank-based as long as their economies are dominated by manufacturing industries. By contrast, the financial system in the United States will continue to be market-oriented as long as service and highly innovative companies constitute a large share of the economy. From the NSFE perspective, although we acknowledge that the industrial structure matters in determining the appropriate financial structure, we further highlight that technological structures are of equal importance. For instance, within the manufacturing sector, some industries are at the global technological frontier, which relies more on capital markets to mobilize large-scale and high-risk capital for innovations, whereas others use mature technologies that may depend on banks for financing.

In summary, although the legal origin, culture, and history play a role in explaining the variation in financial structure, they have limitations in explaining the changes in the financial structure over time. The NSFE draws our attention to the analytical angle of how changes in financing needs of the real economy drive the adjustment in financial systems. This perspective helps to explain the variation in the financial structure across countries and the evolution of the financial structure within a country that are unresolved by the existing theories.

4 Determinants of the Appropriate Financial Structure and Empirical Testing

This section lays out the analytical framework of the NSFE. As emphasized in the Introduction, NSFE maintains that the principal role of finance is to serve the real economy. Hence, to examine the appropriate financial structure, it is important to first analyze distinctive financing needs of the real economy at different stages of development. Then, given the divergent financing needs at different stages of development, we can take a step further to explore comparative advantages of different financial arrangements in meeting the financing demand of the real economy. In contrast with the prevailing view that argues that it is the scale of financial system rather than its structure that matters in promoting economic growth (Levine, 2002), NSFE contends that this strand of literature pays little attention to the distinctive financing demands of the real economy at different stages of development and their implications for the appropriate financial arrangements. In comparison with the mainstream financial service view that emphasizes that functions provided by different financial arrangements are fungible, NSFE argues that one type of financial arrangement may be better positioned to perform a certain function than others as far as specific financing needs of the real economy is concerned. From the perspective of NSFE, only when the supply of the financial structure fits the demand of the

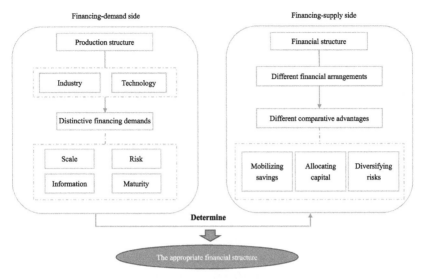

Figure 2 Analytical framework of the appropriate financial structure

production structure can the financial structure be appropriately positioned to serve the real economy (see Figure 2 on the analytical framework of the appropriate financial structure). Given the fact that production structure differs at different development stages, the appropriate financial structure should evolve to meet changing financing needs of the real economy. Hence, NSFE questions the mainstream perspective which contends that there is a one-size-fits-all optimal financial structure for all countries regardless of their stages of development.

In this section, we proceeds as follows: first, we explore how financing demands of the real economy differ at different stages of development; second, we analyze the comparative advantages of different financial arrangements in serving the real economy as far as the distinctive financing needs are concerned; third, we propose how to match the financing demand of the real economy with the supply of financial structure; finally, we make a preliminary discussion on methods about how to empirically test the appropriate financial structure.

4.1 Distinctive Demand of the Real Economy

From the NSFE perspective, grasping the financing needs of the real economy is of paramount importance in answering what the appropriate financial structure is and why there are substantial differences in the financial structure across different countries. This section delves deeper into the distinctive financing needs of the real economy which lays the foundation for examining comparative advantages of different financial arrangements in meeting specific financing needs.

When an economy develops from the early stage to the advanced stage in modern times, the proportion of agriculture in the industrial structure gradually falls, while that of manufacturing and services tends to rise (Kuznets, 1946). During the process, the production structure evolves from labor-intensive to capital-intensive and technology-intensive. Different technologies and industries have different technical features, such as requirements for specific capital, skill and infrastructure, and economies of scale and risk, and thus they have distinctive demands for financing to meet the required size of investment and operation and to cope with the innate risks. For example, Ozawa (2007) noted that the industrial structure of Japan has undergone four stages of development dominated by labor-intensive industries, capital-intensive heavy industry and chemical industry, capital-intensive automobile industry, and R&D-intensive electronic industry, respectively, after World War II. Ju et al. (2015) showed that the capital intensity increased over time within each industry in the United States during the period 1958–2005.

4.1.1 Financing Demand of Developing Economies

At the early stage of economic development, labor-intensive industries are usually prevailing in the production structure. Firms in these industries are often smaller compared with those in capital-intensive industries. For instance, based on the distribution of firm size across industries in fifteen European countries, Kumar et al. (1999) pointed out that the average firm size in capital-intensive industries is larger. Hence, in developing countries, small- and medium-sized enterprises (SMEs) are predominant in production structures (Gollin, 2008; Tybout, 2000).

Firm size matters because it is closely related to the financing scale and information transparency of the firm. Small firms in the labor-intensive industries often require a small amount of external financing owing to the limited scale of investment, production, and sale. Small firms are also more opaque owing to the lack of standard financial information and sufficient credit records compared with large firms with more extended financial history and audited financial statements. Thus, small firms tend to suffer from more severe information asymmetry when seeking external financing.

With respect to the type of risks, firms from labor-intensive industries suffer more from the entrepreneur risk than from technology risk or market risk. Because labor-intensive industries have already existed in developed countries, their technology is relatively mature and the market demand for their products has been tested. Firms in such industries in developing countries can imitate or attract foreign direct investment to learn from the existing technology and managerial experience in developed countries. For instance, the four East Asian Tigers (South Korea, Taiwan, Hong Kong, and Singapore) have utilized their latecomer advantages to achieve rapid economic growth. Compared with original innovation in advanced capital-intensive industries at the global technological frontier, firms in labor-intensive industries can adopt existing technology to produce mature product and face lower technology innovation risk and product innovation risk. By contrast, the entrepreneur risk – that is, uncertainties about managers' ability and integrity – is rife among firms in labor-intensive industries. Exacerbated by information asymmetry, moral hazard problems of managers may be more severe for opaque SMEs. In addition, start-ups are often small businesses wherein managers may lack relevant experience and knowledge in corporate governance, which may result in a higher risk of failure and bankruptcy. Moreover, small labor-intensive firms often have few assets that can be used for collateral.

In short, financing firms in labor-intensive industries from developing economies are characterized by small scale, opaqueness, entrepreneur risks, and often lack of suitable collateral.

4.1.2 Financing Demand of Developed Economies

At the advanced stage of economic development, capital-intensive and technology-intensive industries often account for a lion's share of the production structure. Such industries have distinctive financing demands compared with mature labor-intensive industries. Firms in capital-intensive and technology-intensive industries often require and favor a large amount of external financing for at least two reasons. First, their capital expenditure is large because capital- and technology-intensive firms need to purchase machinery equipment and develop new technology and products. Second, economies of scale can help to save costs and enhance competitiveness. Obtaining external financing entails transaction costs such as expenses on financial audit, information disclosure, and contract negotiation and implementation. Because such expenditures are often fixed, the unit cost of capital will decrease when the amount of financing increases. Thus, large-scale financing is more typical in capital-intensive industries owing to their distinctive financing needs. In addition, a capital-intensive firm's equipment and factory facility are good collaterals.

Furthermore, firms in the high-tech industries usually face significant technological innovation risk and product innovation risk because they engage in research and development as well as innovative activities. The innovation process tends to be idiosyncratic, long term, unpredictable, and with a high probability of failure (Holmstrom, 1989). Such features are more likely to impede effective communication between external finance providers and those firms owing to severe information asymmetry (Bhattacharya & Ritter, 1980). Meanwhile, for firms operating in some new industries, there are still many uncertainties in the product market even if they achieve successful R&D. In fact, it takes time for consumers to be familiar with and develop a taste for brand-new products. Finally, those products might not be accepted by the market, especially when the competition for homogeneous products is fierce.

In summary, the financing demand of firms in developed economies is often characterized by larger scales and higher innovation risks.

4.2 Comparative Advantages of Different Financial Arrangements

Financial institutions serve the real economy by performing functions such as mobilizing savings, allocating capital, and diversifying risks. Different financial institutions have different comparative advantages in performing these functions because they have distinctive organizational forms, modalities, and ways to cope with information asymmetry and moral hazard. As a result, when one financial institution defies its comparative advantages in serving firms or industries, it would undermine the efficiency of this financial institution. For example, if a small bank provides loans to a firm engaging in R&D for a new technology, it will have difficulties to diversify risks. Hence, to enhance the efficiency of the financial system in serving the real economy, it is essential to identify the comparative advantages of different financial arrangements. In the following, we will examine selected financial arrangements to illustrate why different financial arrangements have distinctive comparative advantages.[8]

The remaining section proceeds as follows: we first focus on the widely examined financial arrangements – banks versus the stock market. Then we examine the differences in comparative advantages between big and small banks, and shed light on how digital technology shapes the comparative advantage of digital finance. Finally, we analyze the comparative advantages of informal finance vis-à-vis formal finance in financing the real economy.

---

[8] We assume that the supervision and regulation system is perfect so that financial institutions can efficiently perform their intended functions, because imperfect supervision or regulation may undermine the ability of financial institutions to perform their functions. For instance, some literature highlights the inefficiency of powerful big banks owing to the monopoly when comparing financial intermediaries in a competitive financial market (Rajan, 1992).

4.2.1 Banks Versus the Stock Market

Stock markets are well positioned to diversify risks and finance high-risk projects of technology-intensive industries. In the stock market, investors have full autonomy to allocate their funds. Once investors become the shareholders by purchasing firms' stocks, they will share both profits and risks of firms. Owing to this sharing mechanism, higher expected returns can induce investors to endure higher risks and tolerate short-term failure. Meanwhile, the stock market provides flexible instruments and approaches for investors to diversify and manage idiosyncratic risks, which encourages investors to shift their portfolios toward innovative activities (Levine, 2005). Such features give the stock market advantages in serving innovative firms, which is supported by numerous empirical studies (Brown et al., 2013; Carpenter & Peterson, 2002; Moshirian et al., 2021). Based on cross-country data, Hsu et al. (2014) found that the positive effect of the stock market on economic development is more significant when the industries are more high-tech-intensive in these economies.

Moreover, the stock market is appropriate for large-scale financing of capital-intensive industries. The stock market relies on firms' information disclosure mechanism to mitigate information asymmetry between financers and investors. Information disclosure, however, requires certain fixed costs, such as the expense on the preparation of standard financial annual reports and audits by a third party. The unit cost of capital is high if the amount of financing is small. Hence, it is more suitable for large firms from capital-intensive industries to raise large-scale capital on the stock market owing to the benefits of the economies of scale.

Compared with stock markets, banks have little advantage in serving R&D and innovation activities. Banks raise savings from depositors and grant loans to firms. Firms are obliged to repay the principal and interest on time; otherwise, they would face liquidation if they are on default. Innovative firms tend to lack stable and sufficient internal cash flow to service the debts according to a fixed schedule and hence might face a high probability of liquidation (Brown et al., 2013). Banks often take a conservative attitude toward such innovation projects because they need to ensure repayments on time. Meanwhile, banks do not share the high profits if innovation projects turn out to be successful because firms simply repay principal and interest rates. As a result, banks lack incentives to provide financial support for firms in high-tech industries.

Banks are more suitable for financing small firms in labor-intensive industries. Based on a cross-countries dataset, Kim et al. (2016) found that the relatively small firms grow faster in those countries where banks dominate the financial system. First, banks have the superior ability to harness local information and engage in longer-term relationships with firms, which can alleviate the information asymmetry when funding these small and opaque firms (Sharpe, 1990). In addition, banks can also utilize the collateral to overcome the reverse selection and moral hazard of borrowers (Berger & Udell, 1990). Second, as the specialized financial intermediaries, banks are good at screening and monitoring firms, which is critical to managing entrepreneur risk in these small firms (Chakraborty & Ray, 2006; Diamond, 1984).

4.2.2 Big Banks versus Small Banks

The existing literature suggests that specialization on scale exists in banking, where big banks tend to shun away from small firms but instead focus on big firms, while small banks mainly target small firms (Berger & Udell 1995; Berger et al., 2001, 2005; Huber, 2021). Underlying such a match are significant differences between the two types of banks, especially in diversifying risks, transaction costs, and the way of addressing information asymmetry.

Big banks can often afford large-scale loans for the following reasons. First, big banks have a superior ability to take deposits owing to their widely distributed branches, while small banks tend to focus on the local market with relatively small coverage of businesses. Hence, big banks have more funds to provide to the borrowers than small banks. Second, banks tend to diversify risks by simultaneously serving multiple firms. After the diversification, small banks often struggle to afford large loans, whereas big banks can still provide large-scale loans to big firms.

Meanwhile, big banks favor large firms owing to the transaction cost and information type. First, making a loan, regardless of its scale, usually involves the same routine procedures such as information collection, ex-ante screening, and filling in a similar number of forms. When big banks grant loans to large firms, the unit costs of loans for banks decrease owing to economies of scale. Second, the organizational structure of big banks enables them to better process the hard information. Big banks tend to own multiple layers of management. The lending decisions are often made by senior bank officers in an upper branch rather than by the head of a local branch. Such characteristics of the hierarchy determine that big banks rely more on hard information that can be easily observed, conveyed, and verified (Petersen, 2004; Stein, 2002). By contrast, it is often difficult for small firms to provide standard information. Meanwhile, big firms in general have more assets that can be used for collaterals than small firms. Hence, for big banks, it is more efficient to serve the large firms with sufficient hard information and collateral.

Conversely, small banks have comparative advantages in serving small firms owing to their capability to collect and process soft information. First, small banks are usually involved in frequent and long-term contact with local small firms, which allows them to more easily collect soft information such as entrepreneurs' management abilities and personal characteristics. Second, the organizational structure of small banks is often simple. Hence, they are more capable of harnessing nonstandard soft information. Hence, small banks can assess the credit risks for small firms in a more efficient manner.

4.2.3 Digital Finance and Traditional Finance

Digital finance is the deep integration of finance and digital technology such as big data, artificial intelligence, blockchain, and cloud computing. Research efforts have been made to identify and examine the changes that digital finance brings about in the credit market (Morse, 2015; Thakor, 2020). Tang (2019) found that peer-to-peer (P2P) platform lending, which has surged after the 2008 financial crisis, complements bank lending in terms of small loans. Fuster et al. (2019) documented that the market share of fintech lenders in the mortgage lending market increased from 2 percent to 8 percent during the period 2010–16.

Despite the rapid rise of fintech or P2P lending, the credit extended by traditional financial intermediaries remains predominant (Claessens et al., 2018). From the perspective of NSFE, digital finance and traditional finance are not diametrical, and their relative growth is subject to their comparative advantages and the characteristics of typical firms in the real economy.

Taking the fintech lending and traditional bank credits as an example, one main difference lies in the amount and nature of the information used in the lending decision. Traditional banks tend to rely on standard data such as financial reports and credit history to assess the credit risks and confirm the creditworthiness of borrowers, which usually excludes small opaque firms lacking standard financial information and a track record of credit history. By contrast, fintech companies, which provide loans via big data tools combined with artificial intelligence, are good at gathering and processing borrowers' nonstandard information (e.g., the digital footprints of the individuals or firms while navigating the Internet). With such capabilities, fintech lenders have the comparative advantage in serving small firms, especially those with digital footprints. Thus, when conducting local economic activities with fewer digital records or less access to the Internet, traditional banks are more efficient in providing lending services than fintech companies.

Digital technology can also shape the comparative advantages of traditional banking. As mentioned in Section 4.2.2, big banks tend to be at a disadvantage when funding small firms because they encounter the difficulty of processing soft information. Big banks are also unwilling to finance small firms, because the loan size of small firms is much smaller than that of large firms although both require the same loan approval procedure. Thus, when big banks lend to small firms, they would face higher transaction cost of per unit amount of loan. However, this deficiency can be overcome when big banks invest in and adopt digital technology, which reduces the opaqueness of information and transaction cost. Therefore, big banks can enhance their capability to fund small firms and may be able to provide loans to small firms, which used to be served by small banks. Consequently, the determinant of the appropriate financial structure might change from "firm size" to the "digital endowments" (i.e., the abundance of firms' digital data).

4.2.4 Formal Finance versus Informal Finance

Informal financing generally refers to financing that occurs without a formal financial intermediary between savers and borrowers where there is little reliance on a court of law and little faith in the ability to seize collaterals, including but not restricted to microfinance, trade credit, interpersonal borrowing (money from friends or families), private money houses, pawnshops, and so on, while formal financing mainly refers to banks, stock markets, and bond markets (Allen et al., 2019; Ghosh & Ray, 2016).

Why is informal financing still broadly used despite the injection of formal credit as documented by Siamwalla et al. (1990) and Bell et al. (1997)? One strand of the literature stresses the superior information advantage as well as risk assessment of informal financing through business relations or social networks (Banerjee et al., 1994; Jain, 1999; Stiglitz, 1990; Gine, 2011). For example, Stiglitz (1990) argues that the local moneylenders have more detailed knowledge of borrowers compared with formal financial institutions, which can be used to separate out high-risk and low-risk borrowers and monitor the borrowers more effectively. Another strand of the literature argues that informal financing is the result of financial repression for which formal financing such as commercial banks cannot sufficiently fund some credit-rationed firms, especially small businesses (Bell et al., 1997; McKinnon, 1973; Montiel et al., 1993; Tressel, 2003). As Bell et al. (1997) demonstrate, there will be a spillover of unsatisfied demand into the informal segment of the financing market in response to the extensive credit rationing in the formal segment when governments impose a ceiling on the rate of interest that institutions may charge.

Yet, the existing literature fails to fully explain why informal finance emerged. Financial repression may not be the root cause, since informal financing still widely exists even after the financial liberalization reform in many developing countries. It also fails to explain the limitations of informal finance in serving certain kinds of financing demands. For instance, if informal financing has a superior information advantage compared with banks and equity markets as assumed in the existing theoretical work, why does formal financing such as banks emerge?

From the NSFE perspective, to explain the emergence of informal finance as well as the relative importance informal finance vis-à-vis formal finance one has to consider the characteristics of financing demands in the real economy. Informal finance primarily serves small-scale and relatively low-risk individuals or firms. Informal financing such as trade credit and interpersonal borrowing has advantages in information production and contract enforcement based on closed business relationships or social networks. Take microfinance as an example, which is prevalent worldwide. Microfinance mainly consists of group lending, developed from rotating savings and credit associations (ROSCAs) and credit cooperatives, providing financial services to micro enterprises and poor households that may otherwise lack access to financing with the goal of alleviating poverty and promoting development. Microfinance has comparative advantages in servicing micro enterprises and rural households owing to the jointly liability mechanism – that is, a group of individuals who are familiar with each other within a local region (such as a village) hold joint liability. Micro enterprises and rural households are characterized by extremely small scale and soft information that are hard to verify or transmit. Compared with banks, microfinance is more efficient in preventing the moral hazard of clients (such as micro enterprises and rural households), adverse selection, and enforcement problems (Armendáriz & Morduch, 2000; 2010). Hence, for microfinance, it is efficient to serve micro enterprises and rural households.

However, the size of informal financing and the geographical distance between borrowers and lenders are constrained by the strong reliance on this local information. Meanwhile, informal financing cannot function effectively in a cross-regional manner, that is, to absorb funds in a region and lend to firms or individuals in another region. That's why formal finance such as banks and equity markets emerge. The development of formal finance is endogenous to the increasing demand for large-scale money and high-risk money in order to make up the gaps in informal financing. As for scale, the amount that can be financed from informal sources, especially that from friends and families, is small since these money providers cannot absorb money from the outside in the manner of issuing deposits or securities as the banks and equity markets do. As for risk management, when the risk is relatively low, informal financing can easily handle it by closely monitoring the borrowers. Yet it may not be the case as the risk becomes higher since the money providers of informal financing in a deal are usually composed of only a few individuals and the risk is concentrated. Formal finance such as banks and equity markets can effectively deal with these problems arising from the larger-scale and higher-risk money demand. As can be seen, large banks can provide large-scale loans to large firms that have such demands using the deposits absorbed in different regions, and stock markets can effectively share the risk among a large number of investors.

4.3 Match between the Financing Demand and Supply

The NSFE maintains that an appropriate financial structure matches the financing demand of firms within a certain production structure with comparative advantages of different financial arrangements. Because the production structure varies across different development stages, the appropriate financial structure should differ as well. The appropriate financial structure at the early stage of a developing country should enable financial sectors to meet the demands of labor-intensive industries such as garments and footwear. Firms in these labor-intensive industries are often small, opaque, and with a low-level innovation risk. Owing to the comparative advantages of harnessing soft information, small local banks are more appropriate to provide external financing for such firms. Hence the financial system of a developing country at the early stage should be characterized by the dominance of small banks.

As economies grow, firms in the labor-intensive industries often increase their capital inputs and upgrade their technology level, which induces the emergence of some large-sized enterprises. In this case, big banks and capital markets may emerge. However, such external financing demand is limited because small firms still dominate in the production structure. Hence, small banks will still play a critical role. Meanwhile, technological development might enable those small firms to produce and accumulate certain digital footprints. Under such a situation, small firms can rely on digital finance, such as fintech firms, to seek external finance.

As economies move to the advanced stage, capital-intensive industries and technology-intensive industries dominate. Firms in such industries tend to require large amounts of external financing and face high risks, including technology innovation and product innovation. The stock market and big banks are more suitable to serve those firms, whereas small banks are no longer able to diversify risks and provide large-scale financing. In addition, with the increasing digital level of enterprises, digital finance will play an increasingly significant role. Overall, the financial structure should be dominated by the stock market and big banks in advanced economies.

4.4 A Preliminary Discussion on Methods of Empirical Testing of Appropriate Financial Structure

As already explained, NSFE argues that only when the comparative advantages of financial structure match well with financing needs of the production structure determined by the economy's endowment structure can the financial system effectively perform its functions of mobilizing funds, allocating funds, and diversifying risks so as to contribute to sustainable economic development. Therefore, as the financing needs of the underlying production structure differ, the appropriate financial structure would differ at different stages of development. This section explores how to build on the existing empirical literature to better test the theories on appropriate financial structure.

One strand of the existing literature regresses economic performance on financial structure by using the country-, industry-, and firm-level data. Levine (2002) constructs an assortment of measures for forty-eight countries over the 1980–95 period. The data analysis does not provide any evidence supporting the theories that favor either the bank-based or market-based perspectives. Categorizing countries based on their financial structure does not contribute to explaining the differences in long-term economic performance across nations. Instead, when countries are categorized based on their overall level of financial development, it finds a positive correlation between financial development and economic growth. Beck and Levine (2002) use the data of thirty-six industries in forty-two countries from 1980 to 1990 to empirically test the impact of financial development and financial structure on industry growth and capital allocation. The results show that the overall level of financial development and the legal environment play a crucial role in explaining the differences in the number of establishments within industries that rely on external financing across countries, and the impact of financial structure upon economic growth is not statistically significant. Demirgüç-Kunt and Maksimovic (2002) investigate whether firms' access to external financing to fund growth differs in market-based and bank-based financial systems. Using firm-level data for forty countries, the paper computes the proportion of firms in each country relying on external finance and examines how that proportion differs across financial systems, and finds that the development of a country's legal system predicts access to external finance. Yet there is no evidence that the development of a market-based or bank-based financial system per se affects access to financing. The above literature mentioned in this paragraph assumes that there is an optimal financial structure for all countries. Yet from the NSFE perspective, the potential reason why the coefficient of financial structure is statistically insignificant is that there is no single optimal financial structure for all countries. Hence, statistical insignificance does not necessarily mean that financial structure lacks economic significance.

Another strand of literature holds that the relative importance of banks and financial markets depends on different stages of development. Tadesse (2002) uses a sample of thirty-six countries from 1980 to 1995, and finds that in countries with an underdeveloped financial system, bank-based systems outperform market-based systems. This paper constructs an interaction term between financial architecture and firm size, and then examines the relation between financial architecture and economic performance across countries of differing distribution of firm size, which finds that this correlation is significantly negative in the lowest quartile of countries on the average firm-size scale and significantly positive in the highest quartile of countries. Demirgüç-Kunt et al. (2013) examine the evolving importance of banks and securities markets during the process of economic development. The paper finds that with the growth of economic activities, the association between an increase in real output and that in bank development decreases, while the association between an increase in real output and that in securities market development becomes larger. The results suggest that as economies develop, the services provided by securities markets become more important for economic activity, while those provided by banks become less important.

These efforts have primarily focused on association or correlation between financial structure and economic development, and have not adequately addressed the underlying causal mechanisms. In order to mitigate the potential endogeneity concerns, Allen et al. (2018) conduct event studies using a difference-in-difference strategy, and explore the shocks to the structure of the real economy and investigate how the financial structure responds to such shocks. They use different shocks that alter the economic structures in India, Finland, Sweden, and South Korea. In all these countries the shocks resulted in the significant development of the service sector relative to the industry sector. Consequently, these countries move toward more market-based financial systems. Yet this approach is not free from limitations. First, country selection may not be random. Second, for those policies that cause such shocks, they may not only affect the economic structure but also the financial structure.

To further mitigate the endogeneity problem, structural estimation may be deployed to make the counterfactual analysis to test the causal relationship. Structural estimation is an attempt to estimate an economic model's parameters and assess the model fit, which allows it to answer counterfactual questions such as what would happen if we shocked this variable and how would the world look if we changed this parameter's value. Although strategies such as difference-in-difference, regression discontinuity, and randomized controlled trials have been popular in empirical research in search for robust identification of causal effects, structural estimation can still be a potent complementary tool to help disentangle alternative mechanisms. Especially when there is a lack of data on the treatment or policy we are interested in (e.g., when this policy has never been previously implemented), structural estimation methods may be a viable alternative method of empirical testing.

In addition to enhancing econometric methodology, more efforts can be made to improve the measurement of financial structure. The existing literature mainly follows the approach of Beck and Levine (2002) and Levine (2002) to measuring the size, activity, and efficiency of the financial structure as defined by the relative importance of bank-based versus market-based financial system. This approach provides cross-country data, laying the foundation for empirical analysis. The size of financial structure is a measure of the size of stock markets relative to that of banks, which equals the logarithm of the market capitalization ratio divided by the bank credit ratio. The market capitalization ratio equals the value of domestic equities listed on domestic exchanges divided by GDP, and the bank credit ratio equals the value of deposit money that bank credits to the private sector as a share of GDP. The activity of financial structure is a measure of the activity of stock markets relative to that of banks, which equals the logarithm of the total value traded ratio divided by the bank credit ratio. The total value traded ratio equals the value of domestic equities traded on domestic exchanges divided by GDP. The efficiency of financial structure is a measure of the efficiency of stock markets relative to that of banks, which equals the logarithm of the total value traded ratio times overhead costs. Overhead costs are measured by the overhead costs of the banking system relative to banking system assets. While acknowledging these meaningful efforts, there is room for improvement to address the following limitations of indicators.

First, stock market prices may fluctuate substantially in some years, but this does not indicate that the functioning of the stock market has also changed substantially, nor does it indicate that the financial structure of the country has changed dramatically. This may just be a short-term deviation from the trend. For example, the ratio of US stock market trading value to private sector credit was 1.8 in 2000, and dropped to 0.9 in 2018. Obviously, we cannot think that the importance of the US financial market relative to banks has declined significantly in the past two decades, because the US stock market rose sharply due to the Internet bubble around 2000, and then fell sharply. Hence, we need to explore complementary measures that can mitigate the effect of short-run fluctuations and better reflect the long-term trend of financial structure.

Second, there may be excessive speculation in the stock markets of some countries, resulting in abnormally high values of their financial structures. Take Turkey as an example, from 1999 to 2007; the average value of Turkey's stock market trading value to private sector credit ratio was 2.1, while that of the United States during the same period was only 1.1. It would be misleading to use this measurement to conclude that Turkey's financial structure is more inclined toward market dominance compared to that of the United States. In fact, in most years, the value of Turkey's financial structure is significantly lower than that of the United States.

Lastly, in the case of small economies serving as international financial centers, their stock market trading value to private sector credit ratio can be extremely high. However, the listed companies in these economies may be foreign companies, that is, the highly developed stock market may not mainly serve the financing needs of enterprises within the economy. In other words, existing theories usually assume that the more the financial structure is dominated by the financial market, the more favorable it is for the development of innovative industries in the economy, but obviously this is not fully true for small economies in international financial centers. Taking Hong Kong, China, as an example, from 2007 to 2017, the average ratio of stock market trading value to private sector credit was 3.4, indicating a typical financial structure dominated by the financial market. However, this has not led to rapid development in innovative industries in Hong Kong.

Moving forward, we can at least make two efforts to enhance the empirical testing of appropriate financial structure. First, we can build on the existing static comparative analysis and explore how the change of production structure drives the evolution of financial structure over time. In the future empirical research, we can consider starting from the factor endowment structure and the corresponding production structure to explore the appropriate financial structure. Second, it is useful to explore the conditions under which appropriate financial structure can fulfill its potential for fostering the real economy. The efficiency of financial services for the real economy is affected by transaction costs, market environment, and government governance. Even though a country's actual financial structure is theoretically appropriate, its impact upon economic development may be constrained by institutional environment. For example, the formal or informal systems for determining transaction costs such as corporate information disclosure, qualification review, investor protection, and bankruptcy law will directly affect the efficiency of different financial system arrangements to serve the real economy.

5 The Role of the State in the Financial System

In this section, we examine the role of the state in the financial system. We start with the discussion of the role of governments in addressing market failures with a special focus on PDFIs in case that commercial financial institutions and private capital markets do not meet the financing needs of the real economy, then examine how governments can make tailored financial regulations in line with the characteristics of specific financial arrangements, and finally examine why governments need to take the pragmatic approach to financial reforms rather than adopting shock therapy.

5.1 Establishing PDFIs to Address Market Failures of Financial Markets and Institutions

If the role of finance is to serve the real economy, market failures may exist in decentralized commercial banking systems and private capital markets for serving certain types of investments due to information asymmetry, positive externalities, and excessive risk aversion of commercial financial institutions. Governments may intervene to fix market failures and provide financial support for credit-rationed enterprises or disadvantaged clients such as SMEs and rural smallholders. Government interventions into financial systems can take many forms, including establishing specialized PDFIs, providing state guarantees to incentivize commercial banks to provide financial support for underserved clients, and setting up state-owned venture capital funds to incubate frontier markets.[9] Yet the mainstream perspective holds that governments should not directly intervene in financial systems but rather focus on indirect efforts to enhance the legal and institutional environments (World Bank, 2015). The rationale is that governments may suffer from corruption and rent-seeking so that the cost of government failures may exceed that of market failures. This echoes the debate on industrial policy: even though there is a basic consensus on the necessity of state intervention to address market failures, researchers disagree with each other on how to

---

[9] Sovereign wealth funds (SWFs) are often established by natural resource-exporting countries or countries with a large pool of savings. At first glance, the long-term goals of SWFs seem to fit well with long-term investment needs of developing countries. But unlike DFIs that proactively pursue public policy objectives, including the provision of long-term finance, SWFs are often mandated by governments to make strategic asset allocation to achieve multiple objectives, including intergenerational equity and macroeconomic stabilization. Even though some SWFs have held investments in the infrastructure asset class, it is found that their investments have been primarily commercially driven so that they have typically been focused on bankable infrastructure projects, especially high-return existing infrastructure, rather than greenfield investments. Hence, it is recommended that SWFs should play a complementary role in financing infrastructure rather than duplicating the mandates of development banks (Gelb et al., 2014).

intervene (Lin & Xu, 2018). Although the popular perception that direct state intervention in financial systems fails miserably has tempted us into saying "no" to all kinds of state intervention, a more constructive approach is to delve deeper into comparative studies of both successes and failures to make prudent recommendations on how to make state intervention in financial systems work better in practice. Otherwise, we may risk turning our back on what could be genuinely helpful.

In this section, we will take PDFIs as an example to illustrate why it is important to go beyond unproductive confrontation on whether direct state intervention in financial systems is needed and to investigate how to make it work better. PDFIs are public financial institutions initiated and steered by governments with an explicit official mission to fulfill public policy objectives. In addition to equity- and guarantee-focused public funds, public development banks are a major category of PDFIs. They are potentially useful policy instruments for fixing market failures, incubating markets, and promoting structural transformation in an equitable and sustainable manner. Yet not all PDFIs are successful. It is important to explore how to make PDFIs work better.

The rest of this section proceeds as follows: we will first examine how the prevailing development thinking has shaped the evolution of PDFIs after World War II, ponder what insights the NSFE can offer to study the role of PDFIs, and then introduce the first global database on PDFIs to identify puzzles that the mainstream free-market development thinking fails to explain; we conclude with promising research questions on PDFIs.

5.1.1 A Brief History of PDFIs after World War II

The number of newly established PDFIs exhibits a rise, decline, and renaissance pattern after World War II. In the 1950s, 1960s, and 1970s, structuralism emerged as the first wave of the post–World War II international development thinking. It stressed that the market encompassed insurmountable defects and that a strong government was required to expedite economic development. The slump of international trade in the Great Depression led to export pessimism. Latin American academic elites prescribed the import substitution industrialization strategy (i.e., supporting the development of domestic capital-intensive manufacturing industries to replace foreign imports) as the way for developing countries to rescue themselves from deteriorating terms of trade and avoid being exploited by developed countries. Influenced by the prevailing structuralism that emphasized the dominant role of the government, PDFIs sprang up in the wake of World War II. Developed countries established national development banks (NDBs) for postwar reconstruction, such as Kreditanstalt für Wiederaufbau and Japan Development Bank. Developing countries' governments in Asia, Africa, and Latin America also set up NDBs because they were eager to achieve faster industrialization after gaining their political independence, such as Development Bank of the Philippines (1947), Industrial Development Bank of Turkey (1950), Brazilian Development Bank (1952), and Industrial Development Bank of Kenya (1954), and Nepal Industrial Development Corporation (1959).

However, free-market neoliberalism became the prevailing development thinking after the 1980s and criticized the heavy-handed intervention prescribed by structuralism. It stressed privatization, liberalization, and deregulation to compensate for deficiencies in government failure. In the mid-1980s, debt crises erupted in Latin America and other developing regions. To weather the debt crises, these governments were forced to accept free-market-oriented structural adjustment programs in line with the tenets of the Washington Consensus. Influenced by free-market-oriented neoliberalism, the role of PDFIs was questioned. In this period, academic researchers found rampant government failures. NDBs in developing countries were vulnerable to excessive government intervention, leading to misallocation of resources, towering debts, and corruption (Gordon, 1983; Odedokun, 1996). Owing to the excessive government intervention, development banks were compelled to bail out companies on the verge of bankruptcy falling into the predicament of "soft budget constraint." Worse still, to seek rents, government officials put cheap money from development banks into nepotism-plagued firms with access to funds from capital markets or commercial banks (Ades & Tella, 1997; Claessens et al., 2008; Faccio, 2006). The existence of government failure has been confirmed by the studies on state-owned banks even though their authors did not distinguish NDBs from state-owned commercial banks (Dinç, 2005; La Porta et al., 2002; Levy-Yeyati et al., 2004; Sapienza, 2004). The purpose and role of development banks came into question after the mid-1980s debt crisis. The prevailing economic liberalization forced developing countries to privatize development banks: some were closed or liquidated, and some were merged into commercial banks or investment banks (Bruck, 1998).

However, practices of infrastructure financing have shown that privatization is not a panacea for the effective provision of long-term finance. Commercial banks and capital markets shied away from risky and long-cycle financing projects because they often considered short-term performance or benefits (Kay, 2012). The stringent rules of international development finance constrained the ability of PDFIs to provide long-term finance (Xu & Carey, 2015). Official development assistance also shifted to social sectors such as health and basic education away from infrastructure, placing many developing countries into a growing gap of infrastructure financing (Foster & Briceño-Garmendia, 2010).

Recently, the world is witnessing a renaissance of PDFIs at both the international level and the national level. At the strategy and policy level, international policymakers have placed more and more importance upon PDFIs. The European Union (EU) launched the Investment Plan for Europe in 2014, emphasizing that "effective involvement of National Promotional Banks (NPBs) is necessary to enhance their impact on investment, growth and employment due to their particular expertise and their knowledge of the local context, business and investor communities as well as national policies and strategies" (EU, 2015: 2). The United Nations Industrial Development Organization (UNIDO) formulated a partnership strategy with PDFIs to support larger flows of resources and trigger a stronger impact on the ground (UNIDO, 2014). The United Nations Conference on Trade and Development claimed that "the time is ripe to promote development banks" (2016: 6). The Intergovernmental Group of Twenty-Four on International Monetary Affairs and Development (G-24) and the Global Green Growth Institute have jointly launched the Infrastructure Finance in the Developing World Working Paper Series in an effort to "play a catalytic role in the creation and success of new DFIs."[10] At the practice level, to fill the vast infrastructure financing gaps in developing countries and shape the international development finance system (Xu, 2017), China has taken a leadership role in creating the Asian Infrastructure Investment Bank and the New Development Bank. Both developed countries and developing countries have recently established or plan to establish NDBs. For instance, the UK government established a fully state-owned British Business Bank in 2014, Nepal Infrastructure Bank was set up in 2019, and Development Bank of Ghana was established in 2021.

In summary, PDFIs have undergone three stages of rise, decline, and renaissance under the influence of mainstream development thoughts in the post–World War II era. It seems that neither excessive government intervention nor holistic market-oriented operation yielded the desired development results. On the contrary, they created counterproductive consequences (e.g., corruption, inefficiency, bad debts, and lack of long-term financing). The renaissance of PDFIs calls for new development theories to account for variation in their development performance to avoid historical pitfalls and unleash their full potential.

---

[10] G-24 web. Infrastructure finance in the developing world. [accessed April 14, 2019]. www.g24 .org/infrastructure-finance-in-the-developing-world/.

5.1.2 The First Global Database on PDFIs Worldwide

Despite the renaissance of PDFIs, little systematic effort has been made to identify PDFIs worldwide, let alone gather data on their operation and performance. To fill the gap, the Institute of New Structural Economics at Peking University has initiated to build the first global database on PDFIs worldwide and then collaborated with French Development Agency to construct the database.[11] For the purpose of distinguishing PDFIs from similar institutional arrangements, we propose a set of five qualification criteria that should be met simultaneously to qualify an entity as a PDFI: (1) being a stand-alone entity; (2) using the fund-reflow-seeking financial instruments as the main products and services; (3) having funding sources going beyond the periodic budgetary transfers; (4) having proactive public policy orientation; and (5) having government steering of their corporate strategy. Criterion 1 of being a stand-alone entity is a prerequisite, which helps to distinguish PDBs and PDFIs from government credit programs, trust funds, and special purpose vehicles. Criteria 2 and 3 go a step further to highlight the core features of PDFIs as financial institutions on both asset and liability parts. This helps to distinguish PDFIs from central banks, grant-executing agencies, and aid agencies. Criteria 4 and 5 further highlight that PDFIs are initiated and steered by governments to pursue public policy objectives. This helps to differentiate PDFIs from profit-driven financial institutions and development-oriented financial institutions created by grassroots ventures such as microfinance institutions (Xu et al., 2021).

Based on the firsthand data collection, we have discovered three puzzles that the mainstream free-market development thinking fails to solve. First, PDFIs are not dying out; instead, they are prevalent worldwide. Over 520 PDFIs come from more than 150 countries with aggregate total assets of about 23 trillion USD. Second, not all PDFIs have failed in the past. PDFIs such as Korean Development Bank have played a pivotal role in promoting industrial upgrading and enhancing economic structural transformation. Third, not all PDFIs suffer from poor governance, even if their country-level governance may be poor. These puzzles encourage us to conduct original research to achieve theoretical innovations.

5.1.3 The Insights of NSFE on PDFIs

NSFE is well positioned to develop original theories to unleash the potential of PDFIs for achieving economic structural transformation in an equitable and sustainable manner. From the NSFE perspective, while acknowledging the

---

[11] INSE and AFD, Public Development Banks and Development Financing Institutions Database, www.dfidatabase.pku.edu.cn/.

potential pitfall of government failures, it argues that the role of PDFIs should
not be dismissed without in-depth investigation on why they are needed. To
achieve economic transformation, it is crucial to examine the factor endowment
structure of the economy to identify industries with latent comparative advantage. It is latent because these industries have the lowest factor costs of
production but lack the adequate infrastructure and institution, which results
in relatively high transaction cost, making the industries uncompetitive in
domestic and international markets. To turn the comparative advantage from
latent to real, it is important for governments to play a facilitating role to provide
corresponding infrastructure and institutions to overcome the high transaction
costs due to market failures in making needed improvements in infrastructure
and institution. From the NSFE perspective, PDFIs are potent policy instruments for governments to fill the financing gap where private capital markets
and commercial banks are unable or unwilling to provide financial support.
Compared with direct government interventions into financial systems, PDFIs,
if well governed, may enjoy sufficient professional autonomy to address both
government failures and market failures. Although some PDFIs failed in the
past, one primary reason is that governments pursued the import substitution
industrialization strategy and urged PDFIs to provide cheap credits to capital-
intensive industries that defied comparative advantages. However, despite these
failures, we should not deny the potential role that PDFIs can play in addressing
market failures and improving infrastructure and institutions so as to foster
economic transformation and unleash the potential of latent comparative advantages in line with factor endowment structures to upgrade production structure
in the economy.

Looking forward, it is promising to examine the following research questions
on PDFIs: first, why do governments establish PDFIs? To what extent does the
role of PDFIs adapt to the changing financing demands of the real economy at
different development stages? Second, what accounts for the variation, if any, in
the weight of PDFIs in the financial structure? Third, why do some PDFIs
succeed, whereas others fail in fulfilling their development-oriented mandates?

5.2 Making Tailored Financial Regulations

From the NSFE perspective, there is no universal optimal financial regulatory
scheme for all countries; instead, tailored financial regulation should be made
based on the specific characteristics of financial markets, institutions, instruments, contracts, and so on.[12] In this section, we tentatively explore why

---

[12] The financial service sector has been subject to more extensive regulation than any business
sector other than public utilities in almost every country. The main purpose of financial

financial regulation needs to be tailored by examining distinctive characteristics of stock markets vis-à-vis banking systems, large banks vis-à-vis small banks, commercial banks vis-à-vis NDBs, and formal finance vis-à-vis informal finance.

Regulations of stock markets and banking systems should differ because stock markets and banks function differently. Stock markets create risky liquidity based on money providers' price discovery actions, while banks create safe liquidity by transferring short-term debts such as demand deposits into longer-term assets such as mortgage loans (Dang et al., 2017). Therefore, it is essential to enhance information disclosure in the stock markets through financial regulation. By contrast, banks need to keep the information they produce about backing assets, such as firm loans, secret to maintain outsiders' expectation about the value of banks' debts so that banks' debts (deposits) can be easily traded at par like money because they are "riskless" to some extent. Hence, banking regulation places less importance upon information disclosure and puts more focus on mitigating moral hazards owing to information asymmetry among banks and depositors, such as banks' capital requirements that increase "skin in the game."

Banking regulation should consider how different types of banks can be better regulated. Even though in practice the Basel Accord pays special attention to global systemically important banks, banking regulation has not fully considered the heterogeneity within the banking system. Banking regulation is harmonized across countries even though countries vary in their banking structure, such as a mix of big banks and small banks. For example, although the capital requirements in Basel III were calibrated primarily for big banks in advanced economies, some key emerging-market economies have committed to implementing Basel III, and many other countries are in the process of adopting it to regulate big banks as well as small banks. They do so because they see it as being in their long-term interest even though the standards may pose new risks and challenges (Beck & Rojas-Suarez, 2019), and the Basel Accord has been perceived as the international best practice so that regulators in developing countries face peer pressure to adopt it (Jones & Zeitz, 2017).

It remains unclear whether the regulatory framework designed for big banks is suitable for small banks. Taking capital requirements as an example, the existing literature proposes that when setting capital requirements, regulators should take into account the bank's executive incentive schemes (Eufinger & Gill, 2017), the

---

regulations is to achieve financial stability and efficiency. For example, numerous regulations interfere with the flexible operation of deposit-type intermediaries, such as restraints on the competition for deposits, restrictions on entry, branching and mergers, portfolio regulations, and the system of deposit insurance (Kreps & Chase Jr., 1971).

regulator's screening reputation (Morrison & White, 2005), the bank's ownership structure (Laeven & Levine, 2009), and the country's fiscal capacity (Stavrakeva, 2020). Yet it ignores the substantial difference between big banks and small banks and its impact on the effectiveness of regulatory frameworks. The latest research has begun to pay attention to the importance of bank size. For example, Dávila and Walther (2020) showed that bank size is a key determinant of banks' leverage choices when system-wide bailouts are possible. They argued that the optimal bank regulation should be size-dependent policies where capital requirements are identical for big banks and small banks, but big banks should be charged a supplement tax on borrowing. However, according to Dávila and Walther (2020), the only difference between a big bank and a small bank is that the former is prone to the "too big to fail" moral hazard problem.

From the NSFE perspective, the capital requirements in Basel III may not help small banks to achieve financial stability, given the fact that small banks are generally more opaque than big banks because the former usually lend more to small firms whose information is mainly "soft" (Berger et al., 2005; Huber, 2021; Liberti & Petersen, 2019). Consider a simple case where bank regulations take two forms: capital requirements that specify the level of equity that a bank must hold as a percentage of its total assets, and external regulations that specify the taxation or penalty on the bank if it invests imprudently and such a risk-taking behavior is discovered by the regulator. We argue that the optimal regulations for big banks and small banks should be different – capital requirements for small banks should be higher than those for big banks, and supervising big banks should rely more on external regulation compared with small banks – for the following reasons.

First, big banks have advantages in funding big firms and small banks have advantages in funding small firms owing to the information types of different firms and the organizational structures of different banks (Berger & Udell, 2002; Stein, 2002). Funding big firms usually relies on transaction-based lending technologies such as financial statement lending, asset-based lending, or credit scoring because the information of big firms is mainly "hard" and standard, which is easy to identify, transmit, and verify. On the contrary, loans to small businesses are often relationship-based and rely heavily on "soft" information of small firms that cannot be directly verified by the bank manager who does not produce it. Therefore, big banks of large hierarchies may entail complex agency and information problems when funding small firms because a line manager inside a large hierarchy – who faces the risk that he cannot get a chance to act on his information ex post because he cannot credibly communicate this information to his superior and his effort of producing soft information will be wasted – does less soft information research ex ante (Berger & Udell, 2002; Stein, 2002). Nevertheless, big banks can perform better when funding big firms whose hard information can be easily verified and transmitted. Besides, big banks can serve big firms without syndication because of their higher ability of liquidity production compared with small banks with fewer total assets. The scenarios for small banks are quite different. The agency problem and information problem of small business lending may not be a serious problem for a small bank with few managerial layers, because a line manager who produces soft information may also be in a position to make lending decision, and he will have a strong incentive to gather information ex ante. Therefore, there is an appropriate matching relationship between banks of different sizes and firms of different sizes; that is, big banks fund big firms, and small banks fund small firms.

Second, banking regulation may have a substantial impact on the matching relationship between banks and firms, especially on small banks when they choose which type of firms to fund. When a small bank chooses to fund big firms, it might be the case that small banks can only reach big firms of low quality and high default risk because big firms of high quality and low default risk might have already been funded by big banks. By contrast, when a small bank chooses to serve small businesses, it is more likely to fund small firms of high quality and low risk that are underserved by big banks owing to the difficulty of collecting and transmitting soft information. Besides, small banks are more opaque when providing small business lending or relationship lending based on soft information, which is costly for the "outsider" – the regulator – to verify. As a result, it is hard for the regulator to correctly identify the risk of small banks that serve small firms, let alone impose taxation or penalty on banks' excessive risk-taking behaviors. Therefore, if the external regulation is relatively strict – that is, the taxation or penalty ex post is relatively high – small banks will choose to fund big firms other than small firms, although small banks are more suitable to fund small firms. On the contrary, the taxation ex post on big banks can be high because big banks are more transparent given they mostly fund big firms whose information is mainly hard, and it is less likely for the regulator to wrongly tax big banks.

Nevertheless, bank regulation should not only be limited to capital requirements and external regulation to the excessive risk-taking behavior but also target regulation of other potential risks in banking. For example, stated-owned banks may be inclined to grant loans to politically connected firms, and banks which are controlled by business groups are inclined to provide loans to affiliated enterprises within the business group (Bertrand et al., 2002; Khanna & Palepu, 2000; Khwaja & Mian, 2005). Regulators should mitigate these potential risks by limiting the proportion of bank loans granted to politically connected enterprises, and strictly screening and supervising business groups holding bank shares when issuing banking licenses or approving bank mergers and acquisitions.

When it comes to the question of what the appropriate financial regulatory framework for NDBs is, we would like to investigate whether they should comply with the Basel Accord that was designed to regulate large, complex, and internationally active commercial banks. As discussed, unlike profit-maximizing commercial banks, NDBs are public financial institutions initiated and steered by national governments to fulfil public policy objectives. Unlike retail-deposit-taking commercial banks, NDBs often do not take household deposits; instead, they rely on the government support to mobilize long-term funds via market means, such as issuing bonds on capital markets (Xu et al., 2021).

Although NDBs differ from commercial banks, it is found that a majority of sampled NDBs comply with the Basel Accord or take the Basel Accord as the benchmark to emulate the perceived international best financial regulatory framework. Gottschalk et al. (2022) conducted a survey among fifty NDBs to assess compliance with Basel III. For the purpose of representativeness, the survey took into consideration the income level of their countries, asset sizes, and mandate. Of all the banks included in the survey, nearly 50 percent have answered the questions. Among twenty-four banks, sixteen explicitly acknowledge that they are subject to the same regulatory rules as commercial banks are in their jurisdictions and that these rules are very closely aligned with the Basel Accord. This means that, in that sample, about two-thirds banks are subject to Basel Accord.

From the NSFE perspective, it is of crucial importance to formulate a financial regulatory framework tailored for NDBs to ensure its financial soundness and mitigate the risk of financial crises as financial institutions without undermining their ability to act as development-oriented public financial institutions. Compliance with the Basel Accord may undermine their capacity to fulfill public policy objectives. For instance, Basel credit risk models consider that the longer the term, the greater the risk. But the greater lending periods do not imperatively bring higher risks for NDBs in the same proportion as they do to private banks, because their funding is also held for longer terms such as long-term bonds. Basel III standards on market risks and operational risks impinge on equity finance. But NDBs use equity invest-ments to support innovation, and climate finance, which, in many instances, involves betting on yet untested clean technologies. NDBs often possess industrial expertise to better assess the prospects of emerging industries and technologies. In terms of the capital adequacy requirement, Basel III demands banks to hold higher minimum capital requirements to reduce the risk of insolvency in situations of stress. Basel III has maintained the Basel II minimum capital requirements at 8 percent of risk-weighted assets, but, to that, it has added the requirement of capital conservation buffers at 2.5 percent of risk-weighted assets, to help banks withstand financial distress. For NDBs under Basel III, such standards could also affect disproportionately the availability of credit to those exposures that require more capital. NDBs are often mandated to provide long-term finance such as infrastructure financing, and the empirical study shows that they lend for much longer periods than commercial banks (Hu et al, 2022). But Basel III has in-built features that already require higher levels of capital for longer-term credit. If permission is granted by the national regulator, NDBs with more technical resources and data availability may try to mitigate the quest by adopting internal models for risk assessment. These models permit banks to assign their own risk weights to their portfolio of assets and thereby potentially save capital (Gottschalk et al., 2022).

As for financial regulation of informal finance, NSFE argues that the financial regulation of formal finance is likely to be stricter than that of informal finance, which is also the case in practice (Bell et al., 1997). In the case of informal finance, lenders are often owners of funds. Hence, they have compatible incentives to monitor the behaviors of borrowers. By contrast, in the case of formal finance, banks are often afflicted with the moral hazard problem since the money they lend to firms belongs to depositors. Banks aim to maximize their own profits, not the utility of depositors, and sometimes the two goals conflict with each other. Consequently, the interests of depositors are ranked second, since depositors cannot supervise the bank's behavior in an effective way due to the information asymmetry between the two parties. In general, the larger the size of a bank's liabilities (deposits), the more severe its moral hazard. The scale of formal financing is often larger than that of informal financing. For instance, the size of loans provided by a small bank is generally larger than that of interpersonal borrowing. This entails a stricter financial regulation of banks with a larger size of deposits.

In a nutshell, the appropriate regulation frameworks for banks of different features should differ. As far as the size of banks is concerned, supervising big banks should rely more on external regulation – that is, taxation on the excessive risk-taking behavior – and lower big banks' capital requirements to improve their abilities of liquidation production. For small banks, capital requirements should be higher and external regulations should be less strict so as not to distort the appropriate matching relationship between small banks and small firms. As for NDBs, the compliance with the Basel Accord, which is designed for regulating large and complex commercial banks from advanced economies, would undermine the ability of NDBs to achieve their development-oriented mandate. A tailored regulatory framework is needed to ensure financial soundness of NDBs while unleashing their potential for fulfilling public policies. Regarding the informal finance, the financial regulation of informal finance is likely to be looser than that of formal finance because the lender of informal finance is often the owner of capital and the size of transaction is relatively small.

5.3 Implementing Pragmatic Financial Reforms to Address Financial Depression

Financial repression is the opposite of financial liberalization. It generally refers to a wide array of government policies that restrict the activities of the financial sector; that is, governments interfere with the full potential operation of the financial sector by introducing numerous interventions, regulations, laws, and other nonmarket restrictions to the behavior of banks and other general financial intermediaries. For instance, financial repression includes control on deposits and loan interest rates, exchange rates, and capital accounts; entry and competition in banking; forcing banks (especially state-owned banks) to provide credit allocation to support "leading sectors" (mainly refers to state-owned enterprises (SOEs) or the industries that the government wants to develop); and requiring banks and other intermediaries to hold more government bonds than they would (Chari et al., 2020; Giovannini & De Melo, 1993; McKinnon, 1973; Roubini & Sala-i-Martin, 1995; Shaw, 1973). Countries worldwide, developing countries in particular, have introduced a whole host of restrictions and controls on the behavior of financial intermediaries (Roubini & Sala-i-Martin, 1995).

The existing literature has pointed out that financial repression results in inefficiencies and has made policy recommendations to end financial repression (see Fry, 1980, 1997; McKinnon, 1973; Shaw, 1973). Many developing economies followed these policy prescriptions and removed controls on international asset trade as well as price and quantity rationing in domestic financial intermediation, under the auspices of international financial institutions such as the IMF and World Bank (Giovannini & De Melo, 1993).

However, the results of financial liberalization reforms in many developing countries are disappointing. For example, the IMF and World Bank sponsored the structural adjustment programs since the 1980s, which mainly contained the items of fiscal adjustment, getting the prices right, trade liberalization, and, in general, a movement toward free markets and away from state intervention. A study shows that none of the top twenty recipients of repeated structural adjustment lending, as measured by a total number of adjustment loans from the

IMF and World Bank over 1980–99, were able to achieve reasonable growth. On the contrary, about half of the adjustment loan recipients showed severe macroeconomic distortions (Easterly, 2005). For another example, several Latin American countries such as Chile, Argentina, and Uruguay during the 1970s implemented financial reforms as part of the Structural Adjustment Program to free domestic banks and other financial institutions from government-induced distortions, but these financial reforms yielded widespread bankruptcies, massive government interventions or nationalizations of private institutions, and low domestic savings in domestic financial sectors in the 1980s (Diaz-Alejandro, 1985). Similar results of financial liberalization have been observed in other countries such as Mexico and Russia in the 1980s and 1990s as documented by Arestis et al. (2005).

The frustrating results of financial liberalization sparked widespread discussion about the causes of financial and economic instability (Loizos, 2018). It has been argued that two main factors – macroeconomic fluctuation and institutional underdevelopment – are attributed to instability in these countries when they go through a financial liberalization process. Therefore, the policy implications include two types of policy sequencing – macroeconomic stabilization and institutional development before financial liberalization. For example, McKinnon (1993) proposed to achieve fiscal balance before financial liberalization. It is argued that domestic capital markets should be liberalized, and free international capital mobility should follow once fiscal balance and price stability are established. Mishkin et al. (2003) proposed to establish an effective regulatory and supervisory framework before financial liberalization to avoid financial crises because financial deepening may worsen the problem of information asymmetry without prudential supervision and regulation.

From the NSE perspective, financial repression in developing countries is often endogenous to the distorted production structure. Over the period of the 1950s and 1960s, governments believed in the necessity of development planning as a policy prescription to develop advanced capital-intensive industries for the industrialization and modernization, especially in the so-called backward countries. Giving strong support to this conviction in practice was the seemingly successful experience of adopting the Stalinist system in the Soviet Union during the 1920s and 1930s even as the Great Depression plagued the Western market economies. Therefore, numerous governments introduced interventions and distortions to guide the process of economic development and industrialization after World War II, especially in developing countries. Capital is the most important input and cost for the development of capital-intensive industries. To implement the catching-up development strategy, in the financial sector, many governments imposed interest rate ceilings together with intervention on the credit allocation to support "leading sectors" (Loizos, 2018). Other financial repression policies were also put into effect, albeit with minor variations across countries, such as controls on international capital flows and restrictions on entry and competition in the financial sector.

Financial repression is endogenous to the need for making distorted production structure feasible, which should not be overlooked when implementing financial reforms. Specifically, these "leading sectors" established in developing countries are mainly capital-intensive, not in line with these countries' comparative advantages, and cannot survive without governments' protection and subsidies given the fact that capital is scarce in these countries. As a result, financial repression, such as interest rate controls and other restrictions on financial intermediaries, is treated as an indirect way for governments in these developing countries to support these capital-intensive leading sectors. As a result, these leading sectors can be financed at lower lending rates and with higher credit accessibility than they would be without such policies. The aforementioned argument can shed new insights into the economic instability and financial crisis in these developing countries when they went through a financial liberalization process in the 1970s and 1980s. When focusing on the possibility that financial repression is inherent in the distorted economic structure – that is, to support the nonviable leading sectors from the financial aspect – the radical removal of financial repression will lead to a rapid rise in borrowing cost as well as a decline in the credit accessibility in those leading sectors, resulting in large-scale bankruptcies, stagnant economic growth, and economic instability, as well as financial crises.

As for financial reform, NSFE emphasizes the necessity of identifying the root cause of the distortions in the financial system and implementing pragmatic financial reforms, that is, formulating appropriate financial reform goals and paths. In terms of reform goals, several things should be taken into consideration. The first one is the endowment structure, which specifies the mix of different production factors, such as capital, labor, and natural resources, and determines the (latent) comparative advantages of an economy. The second one is production structure, which specifies the mix of industries/sectors of different capital intensity and technology intensity used in each industry. Financial reform goals should meet the requirements of the real economy, which may differ at different development stages (Allen et al., 2018), rather than blindly treating the financial structure of developed countries as a benchmark and pursuing the so-called advanced financial institutions in developed countries. For instance, if an economy remains in a relatively agriculture-oriented or labor-intensive production structure, it is better for the financial system to be bank-based, and the effort to create or further develop a capital market is not appropriate (Allen et al., 2018).

In terms of reform paths, it is better to implement gradual reforms by taking into account the economy's endowment structure, industrial structure, and nonviable leading sectors' profitability and competitiveness. As for financial repression and financial liberalization, if distortions in the real economy are induced by the nonviability of leading sectors and such sectors cannot be abandoned due to national security or social stability concerns, then it is not appropriate to eliminate financial repression policies – interest rate controls, credit allocations, and so on – simultaneously and aggressively in a short time like the big bang or shock therapy (Lin & Tan, 1999).

China's transition to a market economy is a pertinent example in support of the gradual approach of financial reforms. China introduced its first economic reforms in the late 1970s. At that time, China's production structure was severely distorted because the majority of firms were state-owned, which dominated industrial sectors in every aspect and were mainly either capital-intensive, defying China's factor endowment structure and comparative advantage, or inherited some types of policy burdens, such as employing redundant workers to provide jobs from the previous development planning system. Consequently, these SOEs were nonviable and could not survive without external assistance (Lin & Tan, 1999; Lin et al., 1998). To support these nonviable SOEs for strategic purposes, the government persistently allocated additional credits and provided other assistance through the financial system to the SOEs (Lin & Tan, 1999). That is why a highly centralized banking system was created with strict access restrictions, universal interest rate controls, along with an allocation of credit that was guided by the government to SOEs.

Over the past forty years, China has undergone a spectacular economic and financial transformation involving fast economic growth, sustained capital accumulation, gradual financial liberalization, and sustained financial deepening (Song et al., 2011), in sharp contrast to transitional countries that have introduced "shock therapy." From the NSE perspective, the key ingredient of China's success lies in its pragmatism in both reform goals and reform paths. As for reform goals, China did not take the financial structure of Western industrial countries as its benchmark; instead, China's financial liberalization process had always tried to avoid the collapse of unviable but essential SOE sectors that were established when implementing the heavy industry-oriented strategy from the 1950s to the late 1970s. As for reform paths, the distinctive characteristics of China's transition were "economic reform comes first, and financial reform follows closely" and "feel the stones to cross the river" (i.e., instead of following a blueprint to undertake sweeping reforms, policymakers should pragmatically conduct experiments first to create a feedback loop to adjust the plan). For one thing, China promoted the development of labor-intensive industries that

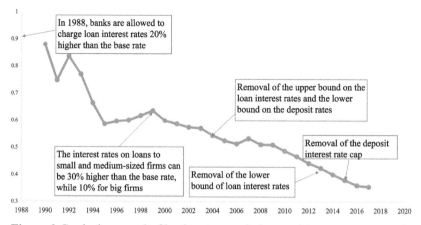

Figure 3 Gradual removal of bank entry restrictions and interest rate controls
and the decline in the banking concentration in China
Data sources: WIND; official website of the People's Bank of China.

were in line with its comparative advantages to accumulate capital, create jobs,
and maintain social stability while still supporting nonviable SOEs through all
kinds of financial repression policies. Capital accumulation under the "dual-
track" reform system induced sustainable changes in China's endowment structure and comparative advantage so that more and more SOEs in the leading
sectors became viable in the competitive market. Later on, as the viability in the
SOE sectors was improved, the government subsidies for SOEs were no longer
necessary. Hence, financial repressions aimed at supporting SOEs also became
unnecessary, and financial restrictions and distortions were eliminated step by
step. For instance, Figure 3 depicts the gradual removal of bank entry restrictions as well as interest rate controls, where the vertical axis represents banking
concentration in China's banking system.[13] As Figure 3 illustrates, between
1990 and 2017, the concentration in China's banking system decreased from
90 percent to 35 percent, and interest rate controls were also eliminated step by
step. In 1990, for example, the total credits of the largest five banks accounted for
88 percent of the entire banking system, and two years before that (in 1988) banks
were allowed to charge loan interest rates 20 percent higher than the base rate for
the first time. In 1999, the fraction of the largest five banks' total credits decreased
to 63 percent, and the interest rate controls were relaxed at the same time; that is,
the interest rate on loans to small- and medium-sized firms can be 30 percent
higher than the base rate and 10 percent higher for big firms. In 2004, the upper
bound on the loan interest rates and the lower bound on the deposit rates were

---

[13] The banking concentration in China is as measured by the ratio of loans issued by the largest five
banks before 2005 and the ratio of assets of the largest five banks after 2005. Due to the limited
data availability, we use two indicators to measure the banking concentration.

removed. In 2013, the lower bound on the loan interest rates was freed, and two years after that the regulator eventually removed the deposit interest rate cap.

China's pragmatic financial reforms have also encountered some difficulties. For example, in 1990s, the stated-owned large banks of China severely suffered from bad loans and fell into the dilemma of technical bankruptcy. The primary cause was that in the late 1970s there remained many SOEs, which were nonviable but inherited some types of policy burdens from the previous state planning system (Lin & Tan, 1999; Lin et al., 1998). To support nonviable SOEs for strategic purposes, the government had to persistently allocate additional credits and provided other assistance through the financial system to the SOEs, so that banking faced high risk of bad loans. Despite these problems, the financial repression under the pragmatic reform has played a significant role in maintaining national defense security, safeguarding national economy and the people's livelihood and maintaining social stability in the early stage of the transition from the planned economy to the market economy. This helps to support economic stability and growth in the long run. By contrast, adopting shock therapy to eliminate the financial distortions is likely to threaten economic and financial stability if policy burdens imposed upon enterprises are not solved. Although it is necessary to adopt a dual-track approach to reforming financial systems, it is important to make timely reforms to gradually liberalize the financial system to solve the problems of bad loans.

In summary, financial distortions or repressions may cause the financial structure to deviate from what is appropriate. From the NSFE perspective, the financial distortion originates from the catching-up strategy of developing capital-intensive industries that defy comparative advantage. Hence, it is necessary for the government to adjust the financial structure through gradually eliminating the financial distortions along with the amelioration of production structure distortions rather than eliminating such distortions overnight.

6 Why Should Excessive Financialization Be Avoided?

In this section, we engage in dialogue with the financialization literature to emphasize that finance should serve the real economy as suggested by NSFE. Broadly defined, financialization refers to the increasing role of financial motives, financial markets, financial actors, and financial institutions in the operation of the economy (Epstein, 2005). Here we primarily focus on the objective of the financial services industry.[14] From the perspective of NSFE,

---

[14] While we primarily focus on the motives of the financial sector, the financialization literature also points out the financial motives behind the real sector and the state. For instance, Demir (2009), Orhangazi (2008) and Epstein and Jayadev (2019) documented the structural change in the portfolio allocation decisions of real sector firms: rather than investing in irreversible long-term

we maintain that the principal role of finance is to serve the real economy by financing productive investments and economic operation rather than indulging in profit-driven arbitrage.

Why is finance inclined to indulge in rent-seeking activities instead of serving the real economy? One reason is that as capital is inclined to seek high returns, credits may be diverted away from productive investments of the real economy and gambled on high-return financial investments. Demir (2009) found that firms may choose to invest in reversible short-term financial investments rather than irreversible long-term fixed investments if the former produce higher returns. Another reason is that loose financial regulation may provide the leeway for financial service sectors to engage in excessive expansion for rent-seeking activities. For instance, one major driving force behind the global financial crisis that erupted in the United States in 2008 is the loophole in financial regulation that resulted in the booming of mortgage securitization. From the NSFE perspective, one potential reason would be the mismatch between financial structure and production structure, which may hinder the role of finance to serve the real economy. For instance, if an economy has a comparative advantage in labor-intensive industries with numerous SMEs but its banking system is characterized by large banks, then SMEs may face credit rationing problems because large banks prefer offering credits to large firms (Lin et al., 2015).

The financial service industry, in a broad sense, mainly includes banking, securities, insurance, and real estate, in comparison with the real economy. The main function of the financial service industry is to reduce transaction costs, improve resource allocation efficiency, and diversify and manage risks to promote the growth of the real economy. However, we sometimes witness an excessive expansion of the financial service industry. Such an excessive expansion of the financial sector may absorb the funds needed for the development of the real economy, resulting in a decline in the investment rate and increase in the operation cost of the real economy. This may even lead to the "hollowing out" of the industry. In the following, we use the examples of the United States and China to illustrate this problem.

Driven by the motivation of maximizing short-term profits, the US banking system suffers from the low efficiency of capital allocation. In the 1970s and 1980s, the US government placed a ceiling upon the interest rate of deposits in commercial banks. However, owing to the high inflation rate, money was

---

fixed investment projects, firms may choose to invest in reversible short-term financial investments. Karwowski (2019) examined the increasing influence of financial logics, instruments, markets, and accumulation strategies in state activities in a way potentially detrimental to the state's accountability toward its citizens.

diverted away from commercial banks in search for high returns. This phenomenon was called "financial disintermediation." In response to the challenge of financial disintermediation, the government has loosened various controls in the financial sector on a large scale, and fierce market competition has formed a wave of financial innovation. Various financial products, financial instruments, and financial organizations have emerged one after another, and the "shadow banking" system has gradually formed in the process. The government-backed Fannie Mae and Freddie Mac and their financial activities have become an important part of the US shadow banking system; they directly catalyzed the US financial bubble, and led to the 2008 financial crisis. In response to the impact of the financial crisis, the Federal Reserve has cut interest rates ten times in a row since August 2007, reducing the federal benchmark interest rate from 5.25 percent in June 2006 to 0.25 percent in December 2008. At the same time, the Federal Reserve has injected a large amount of liquidity into the market to prevent excessive liquidity shortages in domestic and foreign financial markets and financial institutions. However, commercial banks, out of consideration of their own short-term interests and risks, did not fully release liquidity to the credit market but kept the liquidity in the Fed's account. In 2007, US private depository institutions' deposits in the Fed's accounts accounted for only 0.16 percent of their total assets, rising to 5.5 percent in 2008, and then exceeding 10 percent for a long period of time.

Short-term arbitrage in the stock market also reduces the efficiency of market operations and may increase financial risks. As a common method in full-fledged capital markets, share repurchase is widely used to optimize capital structure, enhance company value, or send positive signals when a company's share price is undervalued. After 2009, the scale of US stock repurchases increased significantly, especially for large leading companies, mainly technology and financial companies. After 2009, bond interest rates fell sharply, and the cost of debt financing was significantly reduced, which stimulated a large number of listed companies to increase debt financing. However, the funds obtained from debt financing did not form new investments but were largely used to repurchase their own companies' shares, which directly pushed up their own companies' stock price. Instead of benefiting most Americans, share buybacks have instead boosted stock prices, leaving most of the benefits to shareholders and corporate executives, further widening the gap between the rich and the poor. In addition, stock buybacks limit the ability of companies to reallocate profits in R&D, equipment, salary enhancements, employee training, pensions, and so on and are not conducive to long-term business growth. Stockhammer (2004) noted that higher financial profits and changes in corporate governance lead to changes in management priorities and incentives. As a result of these institutional changes, managements of nonfinancial corporations have begun to adopt financial market preferences, which focus on short-term returns rather than long-term growth. This change in management's preference has had a negative impact on actual investment, in that managements of non-financial firms now have fewer long-term growth-oriented priorities, opting instead to increase financial investments in their firms.

If finance indulges in rent-seeking activities, it can spawn financial crises. Minsky maintains that the financial system tends to move from stability to fragility to crisis, and the point before a complete market collapse is called the "Minsky Moment." Minsky argues that the true essence of capitalism is its tendency to expand, accompanied by endogenous fragility and financial crises: when the economy is booming, investors take risks; the longer the boom lasts, the more investors take risks, and the more leveraged investors become until they over-risk. In such circumstances, investors will reach a tipping point where their assets no longer generate enough cash to pay off the debts they have taken on, and the loss of speculative assets will prompt lenders to take back their loans. Once a significant portion of investors in the economy are facing default on their debts, the chain reaction manifests itself in a macroeconomic crisis, asset prices fall sharply until they collapse, and a Minsky moment occurs (Minsky, 2008). One notorious source of financial instability is Ponzi schemes, whose organizers often promise to invest the money of investors and generate high returns with little or no risk. Yet, in fact, it is an investment fraud that pays existing investors with funds collected from new investors. With the deregulation of finance in the 1980s, the financialization of the US economy accelerated and led to increased instability in the financial system and frequent financial crises. As a result, Minsky explicitly opposed some financial deregulation in the 1980s, supported some government intervention in financial markets, and emphasized the importance of the Federal Reserve as the lender of last resort (Minsky,1993).

If commercial banks engage in short-term arbitrage, they may divert their funds away from supporting the real economy. Taking China's bank-ing system as an example, the return on investment in China's real econ-omy has declined since the financial crisis of 2008. Commercial banks have been unwilling to assume higher risks in traditional credit business and have preferred lending funds to financial institutions to secure low-risk profits. Consequently, this phenomenon has led to a significant problem of capital idling within China's financial system. Figure 4 illustrates the widening gap between total bank deposits and total bank loans since 2008. In response to this issue, the China Banking Regulatory

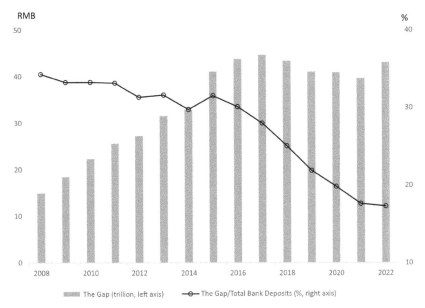

Figure 4 Evolution of the gap between total bank deposits and total bank loans in China

Data Source: The National Administration of Financial Regulation of China

Commission[15] has taken a series of activities to strengthen banking supervision since 2017.[16] These interventions have played a crucial role in stemming the trend of diverting funds away from financing the real economy.

To mitigate the problem that finance is diverted from serving the real economy, governments can play an indispensable role in enhancing the match between financial structure and the production structure, enabling industrial upgrading, and strengthening financial regulation to guide finance to better serve the real economy. First, governments can play a facilitating role in enhancing the match between financial structure and production structure. To unleash the potential of the financial service sectors in serving the real economy, they need to meet the financing demands of the production structure in line with comparative advantages. Yet sometimes governments may adopt an overly ambitious catching-up strategy, which results in distortion in the production

---

[15] In 2018, the China Banking Regulatory Commission and the China Insurance Regulatory Commission were merged to form the China Banking and Insurance Regulatory Commission. In 2023, the China Banking and Insurance Regulatory Commission was integrated into the National Administration of Financial Regulation. The establishment of the new regulator is expected to strengthen and improve the country's financial regulation.

[16] For instance, in 2017, the China Banking Regulatory Commission launched the special rectification campaign. After this campaign, the interbank liabilities of the banking industry shrank by more than one trillion RMB, www.gov.cn/xinwen/2018-01/22/content_5259163.htm for details.

structure. To improve the efficiency of finance, governments need to first address the distortion in the production structure and then match it with the appropriate financial structure. Meanwhile, developing country governments should not blindly copy the financial structure of advanced economies because their underlying production structures are different. Hence, governments should diagnose causes of mismatch between financial structure and production structure and make efforts to address the mismatch. Second, governments should play a facilitating role in promoting industrial upgrading and technological progress so that credits would be channeled to long-term productive investments rather than indulging in short-term arbitrage. Third, governments should strengthen the financial regulation to incentivize financial institutions to better serve the real economy while maintaining the financial stability. Governments need to strike the right balance between fostering financial innovation and maintaining financial stability. Different financial institutions may encounter different types of risks; hence, governments should tailor their financial regulatory framework to unleash the potential of financial service sectors for serving the real economy while avoiding indulging in short-term arbitrage.

7 Conclusion

Centering around the core issue of how finance better serves the real economy, in this Element we propose the foundation and analytical framework of NSFE as an alternative theoretical perspective on how to make finance better serve the real economy. It has three propositions.

First, an examination of the appropriate financial structure should take the economy's production structure as the starting point of analysis. The mainstream economics takes the economic structure of developed countries as the benchmark and neglects structural differences between developing countries and developed countries. NSE maintains that the factor endowment structure endogenously determines the production structure, which in turn endogenously determines the infrastructure and the superstructure of the economy.

Second, the appropriate financial structure, which is a component in the superstructure, is endogenously determined by the needs of the prevailing production structure. The principal role of finance is to serve the real economy to facilitate economic operation, increase productivity, promote industrial upgrading, and foster technological progress. Financing needs of the real economy differ substantially in terms of the scale, maturity, risks, and information asymmetry at different stages of development. Meanwhile, different financial institutions have distinctive comparative advantages in serving the financing needs with different characteristics. Hence, an appropriate financial structure needs to match divergent financing needs with distinctive financial arrangements.

Third, a government should tailor financial regulation, play a proactive role to optimize the financial structure in case of market failures, and adopt pragmatic financial reforms in line with the financing needs of its real economy at different development and transition stages. While acknowledging the possibility of government failures, NSFE proposes that governments should proactively fix market failures and provide financial support for credit-rationed enterprises or disadvantaged clients such as SMEs and rural smallholders. One key way of government interventions is to establish PDFIs with the official mandate to fulfill public policy objectives. It is important to examine the conditions under which government intervention to optimize financial structure can be effective to avoid pitfalls of government failures. Regarding the financial regulation, NSFE argues that there is no optimal uniform financial regulatory scheme for all countries; instead, tailored financial regulation should be made based on the specific characteristics of financial markets, institutions, instruments, contracts, and so on. Finally, NSFE cautiously question the virtue of eradicating financial repressions in a sweeping manner, because financial repression in many developing countries is often endogenous to the distorted production structure as a result of ambitious catching-up development strategies to develop capital-intensive industries that defy the economy's comparative advantage but are important for national security and maintaining social stability in economic transition. Hence, it is necessary for the government to adjust the financial structure through gradually eliminating the financial distortions rather than eliminating such distortions overnight.

These theoretical insights provide alternative perspectives on the key research questions of what determines the appropriate financial structure in an economy, what are the determinants of financial structure and its evolution in an economy, and what the adequate role of state in the determination of financial system and its evolution is and how to enhance it. More efforts can be made to develop rigorous theoretical models and conduct empirical studies to test and further develop these theoretical insights.

References

Ades, A., & Tella, R. D. (1997). National champions and corruption: Some unpleasant interventionist arithmetic. *The Economic Journal*, 107(443), 1023–1042.

Allen, F., & Gale, D. (1999). Diversity of opinion and financing of new technologies. *Journal of Financial Intermediation*, 8(1–2), 68–89.

Allen, F., & Gale, D. (2000). Financial contagion. *Journal of Political Economy*, 108(1), 1–33.

Allen, F., Bartiloro, L., Gu, X., & Kowalewski, O. (2018). Does economic structure determine financial structure? *Journal of International Economics*, 114, 389–409.

Allen, F., Qian, M., & Xie, J. (2019). Understanding informal financing. *Journal of Financial Intermediation*, 39, 19–33.

Arestis, P., Nissanke, M., & Stein, H. (2005). Finance and development: Institutional and policy alternatives to financial liberalization theory. *Eastern Economic Journal*, 31(2), 245–263.

Armendáriz de Aghion, B., & Morduch, J. (2000). Microfinance beyond group lending. *Economics of Transition*, 8(2), 401–420.

Armendáriz de Aghion, B., & Morduch, J. (2010). *The Economics of Microfinance*. Cambridge, MA: Massachusetts Institute of Technology Press.

Banerjee, A. V., Besley, T., & Guinnane, T. W. (1994). Thy neighbor's keeper: The design of a credit cooperative with theory and a test. *Quarterly Journal of Economics*, 109(2), 491–515.

Beck, T., & Levine, R. (1999). *A New Database on Financial Development and Structure* (Vol. 2146). Washington, DC: World Bank.

Beck, T., & Levine, R. (2002). Industry growth and capital allocation: Does having a market-or bank-based system matter? *Journal of Financial Economics*, 64(2), 147–180.

Beck, T., & Rojas-Suarez, L. (2019). *Making Basel III Work for Emerging Markets and Developing Economies: A CGD Task Force Report*. Available at SSRN 3391886.

Beck, T., Demirgüç-Kunt, A., & Maksimovic, V. (2004). Bank competition and access to finance: International evidence. *Journal of Money, Credit and Banking*, 36(3), 627–648.

Bell, C., Srintvasan, T. N., & Udry, C. (1997). Rationing, spillover, and inter-linking in credit markets: The case of rural Punjab. *Oxford Economic Papers*, 49(4), 557–585.

Berger, A. N., & Udell, G. F. (1990). Collateral, loan quality and bank risk. *Journal of Monetary Economics*, 25(1), 21–42.

Berger, A. N., & Udell, G. F. (1995). Relationship lending and lines of credit in small firm finance. *Journal of Business*, 68(3), 351–381.

Berger, A. N., & Udell, G. F. (2002). Small business credit availability and relationship lending: The importance of bank organisational structure. *The Economic Journal*, 112(477), F32–F53.

Berger, A. N., Klapper, L. F., & Udell, G. F. (2001). The ability of banks to lend to informationally opaque small businesses. *Journal of Banking & Finance*, 25(12), 2127–2167.

Berger, A. N., Miller, N. H., Petersen, M. A., Rajan, R. G., & Stein, J. C. (2005). Does function follow organizational form? Evidence from the lending practices of large and small banks. *Journal of Financial Economics*, 76(2), 237–269.

Bertrand, M., Mehta, P., & Mullainathan, S. (2002). Ferreting out tunneling: An application to Indian business groups. *The Quarterly Journal of Economics*, 117(1), 121–148.

Bhattacharya, S., & Ritter, J. R. (1980). Innovation and communication: Signaling with partial disclosure. *Journal of Financial and Quantitative Analysis*, 15(4), 853–854.

Bodie, Z., & Merton, R. C. (1998). *Finance*. Upper Saddle River, NJ: Prentice Hall.

Boyd, J. H., & Smith, B. D. (1998). The evolution of debt and equity markets in economic development. *Economic Theory*, 12, 519–560.

Brown, J. R., Martinsson, G., & Petersen, B. C. (2013). Law, stock markets, and innovation. *The Journal of Finance*, 68(4), 1517–1549.

Bruck, N. (1998). Role of development banks in the twenty-first century. *Journal of Emerging Markets*, 3, 39–68.

Cameron, R. (1992). *Financing Industrialization*. Aldershot: Edward Elgar.

Cameron, R., Crisp, O., Patrick, H. T., & Tilly, R. (1967). *Banking in the Early Levels of Industrialization*. New York: Oxford University Press.

Carpenter, R. E., & Petersen, B. C. (2002). Is the growth of small firms constrained by internal finance? *Review of Economics and Statistics*, 84(2), 298–309.

Chakraborty, S., & Ray, T. (2006). Bank-based versus market-based financial systems: A growth-theoretic analysis. *Journal of Monetary Economics*, 53(2), 329–350.

Chari, V. V., Dovis, A., & Kehoe, P. J. (2020). On the optimality of financial repression. *Journal of Political Economy*, 128(2), 710–739.

Claessens, S., Coleman, N., & Donnelly, M. (2018). "Low-for-long" interest rates and banks' interest margins and profitability: Cross-country evidence. *Journal of Financial Intermediation*, 35, 1–16.

Claessens, S., Feijen, E., & Laeven, L. (2008). Political connections and preferential access to finance: The role of campaign contributions. *Journal of Financial Economics*, 88(3), 554–580.

Collins, M. (1988). *Money and Banking in the UK*. New York: Croom Helm.

Cull, R., Davis, L. E., Lamoreaux, N. R., & Rosenthal, J. L. (2006). Historical financing of small and medium-size enterprises. *Journal of Banking & Finance*, 30(11), 3017–3042.

Cull, R., Demirguc-Kunt, A., & Lin, J. Y. (2013). Financial structure and economic development: A reassessment. *World Bank Economic Review*, 27(3), 470–475.

Dang, T. V., Gorton, G., Holmström, B., & Ordonez, G. (2017). Banks as secret keepers. *American Economic Review*, 107(4), 1005–1029.

Dávila, E., & Walther, A. (2020). Does size matter? Bailouts with large and small banks. *Journal of Financial Economics*, 136(1), 1–22.

Demir, F. (2009). Financial liberalization, private investment and portfolio choice: Financialization of real sectors in emerging markets. *Journal of Development Economics*, 88(2), 314–324.

Demirgüç-Kunt, A., & Maksimovic, V. (2002). Funding growth in bank-based and market-based financial systems: Evidence from firm-level data. *Journal of Financial Economics*, 65(3), 337–363.

Demirgüç-Kunt, A., Feyen, E., & Levine, R. (2011). Optimal financial structures and development: The evolving importance of banks and markets. World Bank Policy Research Working Paper No. 5805.

Demirgüç-Kunt, A., Feyen, E., & Levine, R. (2013). The evolving importance of banks and securities markets. *The World Bank Economic Review*, 27(3), 476–490.

Diamond, D. W. (1984). Financial intermediation and delegated monitoring. *The Review of Economic Studies*, 51(3), 393–414.

Diaz-Alejandro, C. (1985). Good-bye financial repression, hello financial crash. *Journal of Development Economics*, 19(1–2), 1–24.

Dinç, I. S. (2005). Politicians and banks: Political influences on government-owned banks in emerging markets. *Journal of Financial Economics*, 77(2), 453–479.

Easterly, W. (2005). What did structural adjustment adjust?: The association of policies and growth with repeated IMF and World Bank adjustment loans. *Journal of Development Economics*, 76(1), 1–22.

Epstein, G. A. (2005). *Financialization and the World Economy*. Aldershot: Edward Elgar.

Epstein, G. A., & Jayadev, A. (2019). The rise of rentier incomes in OECD countries: Financialization, central bank policy and labor solidarity. In G. A. Epstein, ed., *Financialization and the World Economy*. Cheltenham: Elgar, pp. 350–378.

European Commission. (2015). Working together for jobs and growth: The role of National Promotional Banks (NPBs) in supporting the Investment Plan for Europe. Brussels: European Commission. Communication from the Commission to the European Parliament and the Council. https://data.con silium.europa.eu/doc/document/ST-11283-2015-INIT/en/pdf.

Eufinger, C., & Gill, A. (2017). Incentive-based capital requirements. *Management Science*, 63(12), 4101–4113.

Faccio, M. (2006). Politically connected firms. *American Economic Review*, 96(1), 369–386.

Foster, V., & Briceño-Garmendia, C. (2010). *Africa's Infrastructure: A Time forTransformation*. Washington, DC: World Bank.

Fry, M. J. (1980). Saving, investment, growth and the cost of financial repression. *World Development*, 8(4), 317–327.

Fry, M. J. (1997). In favour of financial liberalisation. *The Economic Journal*, 107(442), 754–770.

Fuster, A., Plosser, M., Schnabl, P., & Vickery, J. (2019). The role of technology in mortgage lending. *The Review of Financial Studies*, 32(5), 1854–1899.

Gelb, A., Tordo, S., Halland, H., Arfaa, N., & Smith, G. (2014). Sovereign wealth funds and long-term development finance: Risks and opportunities. Washington D.C.: World Bank Policy Research Working Paper No. 6776.

Ghosh, P., & Ray, D. (2016). Information and enforcement in informal credit markets. *Economica*, 83(329), 59–90.

Gine, X. (2011). Access to capital in rural Thailand: An estimated model of formal vs. informal credit. *Journal of Development Economics*, 96(1), 16–29.

Giovannini, A., & De Melo, M. (1993). Government revenue from financial repression. *American Economic Review*, 83(4), 953–963.

Goldsmith, R. W. (1969). *Financial Structure and Development*. New Haven, CT: Yale University Press.

Gollin, D. (2008). Nobody's business but my own: Self-employment and small enterprise in economic development. *Journal of Monetary Economics*, 55(2), 219–233.

Gong, D., Xu, J., & Yan, J. (2023). National development banks and loan contract terms: Evidence from syndicated loans. *Journal of International Money and Finance*, 130, 102763. https://doi.org/10.1016/j.jimonfin.2022.102763.

Gordon, D. L. (1983). *Development Finance Companies, State and Privately Owned*. Washington, DC: The World Bank.

Gottschalk, R., Castro, L. B., & Xu, J. (2022). Should national development banks be subject to Basel III? *Review of Political Economy*, 34(2), 249–267.

Hausmann, R., Klinger, B., & Wagner, R. (2008). Doing growth diagnostics in practice: A "mindbook." CID Working Paper Series 2008.177, Cambridge, MA: Harvard University.

Hausmann, R., Rodrik, D., & Velasco, A. (2005): Growth diagnostics. Unpublished manuscript, Inter-American Development Bank.

Holmstrom, B. (1989). Agency costs and innovation. *Journal of Economic Behavior & Organization*, 12(3), 305–327.

Holmstrom, B., & Tirole, J. (1993). Market liquidity and performance monitoring. *Journal of Political Economy*, 101(4), 678–709.

Holmstrom, B., & Tirole, J. (1997). Financial intermediation, loanable funds, and the real sector. *The Quarterly Journal of Economics*, 112(3), 663–691.

Hsu, P. H., Tian, X., & Xu, Y. (2014). Financial development and innovation: Cross-country evidence. *Journal of Financial Economics*, 112(1), 116–135.

Hu, B., Schclarek, A., Xu, J., & Yan, J. (2022). Long-term finance provision: National development banks vs commercial banks. *World Development*, 158, 105973. https://doi.org/10.1016/j.worlddev.2022.105973.

Huber, K. (2021). Are bigger banks better? Firm-level evidence from Germany. *Journal of Political Economy*, 129(7), 2023–2066.

Jain, S. (1999). Symbiosis vs. crowding-out: The interaction of formal and informal credit markets in developing countries. *Journal of Development Economics*, 59(2), 419–444.

Jensen, M. C., & Meckling, W. H. (1976). Theory of the firm: Managerial behavior, agency costs and ownership structure. *Journal of Financial Economics*, 3(4), 305–360.

Jensen, M. C., & Murphy, K. J. (1990). Performance pay and top-management incentives. *Journal of Political Economy*, 98(2), 225–264.

Jones, E., & Zeitz, A. O. (2017). The limits of globalizing Basel banking standards. *Journal of Financial Regulation*, 3(1), 89–124.

Ju, J, Lin, J. Y., & Wang, Y. (2015). Endowment structures, industrial dynamics, and economic growth. *Journal of Monetary Economics*, 76, 244–263.

Karwowski, E. (2019). Towards (de-) financialisation: The role of the state. *Cambridge Journal of Economics*, 43(4), 1001–1027.

Kay, J. (2012). The Kay review of UK equity markets and long-term decision making. https://webarchive.nationalarchives.gov.uk/ukgwa/20121204 143307mp_/, www.bis.gov.uk/assets/BISCore/business-law/docs/K/12-917-kay-review-of-equity-markets-final-report.pdf.

Khanna, T, & Palepu K. (2000). Is group affiliation profitable in emerging markets? An analysis of diversified Indian business groups. *The Journal of Finance*, 55(2), 867–891.

Khwaja, A. I., & Mian, A. (2005). Do lenders favor politically connected firms? Rent provision in an emerging financial market. *The Quarterly Journal of Economics*, 120(4), 1371–1411.

Kim, D. H., Lin, S. C., & Chen, T. C. (2016). Financial structure, firm size and industry growth. *International Review of Economics & Finance*, 41, 23–39.

Kreps, C. H., & Chase Jr., S. B. (1971). Financial structure and regulation: Some knotty problems. *The Journal of Finance*, 26(2), 585–598.

Kumar, K., Rajan, R., & Zingales, L. (1999). *What Determines Firm Size?* Cambridge, MA: NBER Working Paper No. 7208.

Kuznets, S. (1946). *National Product since 1869*, New York: National Bureau of Economic Research.

Kwok, C. C., & Tadesse, S. (2006). National culture and financial systems. *Journal of International Business Studies*, 37(2), 227–247.

La Porta, R., Lopez-de-Silanes, F., & Shleifer, A. (2002). Government ownership of banks. *The Journal of Finance*, 57(1), 265–301.

La Porta, R., Lopez-de-Silanes, F., Shleifer, A., & Vishny, R. W. (1997). Legal determinants of external finance. *The Journal of Finance*, 52(3), 1131–1150.

La Porta, R., Lopez-de-Silanes, F., Shleifer, A., & Vishny, R. W. (1998). Law and finance. *Journal of Political Economy*, 106(6), 1113–1155.

Laeven, L., & Levine, R. (2009). Bank governance, regulation and risk taking. *Journal of Financial Economics*, 93(2), 259–275.

Levine, R. (1991). Stock markets, growth, and tax policy. *The Journal of Finance*, 46(4), 1445–1465.

Levine, R. (1997). Financial development and economic growth: Views and agenda. *Journal of Economic Literature*, 35(2), 688–726.

Levine, R. (2002). Bank-based or market-based financial systems: Which is better?. *Journal of Financial Intermediation*, 11(4), 398–428.

Levine, R. (2005). Finance and growth: Theory and evidence. *Handbook of Economic Growth*, 1, 865–934.

Levy-Yeyati, E. L., Micco, A., & Panizza, U. (2004). *Should the Government be in the Banking Business? The Role of State-Owned and Development Banks*. Washington, D.C.: Inter-American Development Bank Working Paper No. 517.

Liberti, J. M., & Petersen, M. A. (2019). Information: Hard and soft. *Review of Corporate Finance Studies*, 8(1), 1–41.

Lin, J. Y. (1989). An economic theory of institutional change: Induced and imposed change. *Cato Journal*, 9, 1–33

Lin, J. Y. (2012). *New Structural Economics: A Framework for Rethinking Development*. Washington, DC: The World Bank.

Lin, J. Y., & Tan, G. (1999). Policy burdens, accountability, and the soft budget constraint. *American Economic Review*, 89(2), 426–431.

Lin, J. Y., & Xu, J. (2018). Rethinking industrial policy from the perspective of new structural economics. *China Economic Review*, 48, 155–157.

Lin, J. Y., Cai, F., & Li, Z. (1998). Competition, policy burdens, and state-owned enterprise reform. *The American Economic Review*, 88(2), 422–427.

Lin, J. Y., Sun, X., & Jiang, Y. (2013). Endowment, industrial structure, and appropriate financial structure: A new structural economics perspective. *Journal of Economic Policy Reform*, 16(2), 109–122.

Lin, J. Y., Sun, X., & Wu, Harry X. (2015). Banking structure, labor intensity, and industrial growth: Evidence from China. *Journal of Banking & Finance*, 58, 131–143.

Loizos, K. (2018). The financial repression-liberalization debate: Taking stock, looking for a synthesis. *Journal of Economic Surveys*, 32(2), 440–468.

McKinnon, R. (1973). *Money and Capital in Economic Development*. Washington, DC: The Brookings institute.

McKinnon, R. I. (1993). *The Order of Economic Liberalization: Financial Control in the Transition to a Market Economy*. Washington, DC: Johns Hopkins University Press.

Merton, R. C. (1995). A functional perspective of financial intermediation. *Financial Management*, 24(2), 23–41.

Merton, R. C., & Bodie, Z. (2006). Design of financial systems: Towards a synthesis of function and structure. *Journal of Investment Management*, 3(1), 1–27.

Miao, M., Niu, G., & Noe, T. (2021). Contracting without contracting institutions: The trusted assistant loan in 19th century China. *Journal of Financial Economics*, 140(3), 987–1007.

Minsky, H. P. (1993). Finance and stability: The limits of capitalism. Annandale-on-Hudson, New York: Levy Economics Institute Working Paper No. 93.

Minsky, H. P. (2008). *Stabilizing an Unstable Economy*. New York: McGraw Hill.

Mishkin, F. S., Crockett, A., Dooley, M. P., & Ahluwalia, M. S. (2003). Financial policies. In M. Feldstein, ed., *Economic and Financial Crises in Emerging Market Economies*. Chicago: University of Chicago Press, pp. 93–154.

Modigliani, F., & Miller, M. H. (1958). The cost of capital, corporation finance and the theory of investment. *The American Economic Review*, 48(3), 261–297.

Monnet, C., & Quintin, E. (2007). Why do financial systems differ? History matters. *Journal of Monetary Economics*, 54(4), 1002–1017.

Montiel, P., Agenor, P. R., & Haque, N. U. (1993). *Informal Financial Markets in Developing Countries*. Cambridge: Blackwell.

Morrison, A. D., & White, L. (2005). Crises and capital requirements in banking. *American Economic Review*, 95(5), 1548–1572.

Morse, A. (2015). Peer-to-peer crowdfunding: Information and the potential for disruption in consumer lending. *Annual Review of Financial Economics*, 7, 463–482.

Moshirian, F., Tian, X., Zhang, B., & Zhang, W. (2021). Stock market liberalization and innovation. *Journal of Financial Economics*, 139(3), 985–1014.

Myers, S. C. (2001). Capital structure. *Journal of Economic Perspectives*, 15(2), 81–102.

Odedokun, M. O. (1996). International evidence on the effects of directed credit programmes on efficiency of resource allocation in developing countries: The case of development bank lendings. *Journal of Development Economics*, 48(2), 449–460.

Orhangazi, Ö. (2008). Financialisation and capital accumulation in the non-financial corporate sector: A theoretical and empirical investigation on the US economy: 1973–2003. *Cambridge Journal of Economics*, 32(6), 863–886.

Ozawa, T. (2007). *Institutions, Industrial Upgrading, and Economic Performance in Japan: The Flying-Geese Paradigm of Catch-up Growth*. Northampton, MA: Edward Elgar.

Petersen, M. A. (2004). Information: Hard and soft. *The Review of Corporate Finance Studies*, 8(1), 1–41.

Rajan, R. G. (1992). Insiders and outsiders: The choice between informed and arm's-length debt. *The Journal of Finance*, 47(4), 1367–1400.

Rajan, R. G., & Zingales, L. (1998). Financial dependence and growth. *American Economic Review*, 88, 559–586

Rajan, R. G., & Zingales, L. (2003). The great reversals: The politics of financial development in the twentieth century. *Journal of Financial Economics*, 69(1), 5–50.

Roubini, N., & Sala-i-Martin, X. (1995). A growth model of inflation, tax evasion, and financial repression. *Journal of Monetary Economics*, 35(2), 275–301.

Sapienza, P. (2004). The effects of government ownership on bank lending. *Journal of Financial Economics*, 72(2), 357–384.

Schclarek, A., Xu, J., & Yan, J. (2023). The maturity-lengthening role of national development banks. *International Review of Finance*, 23(1), 130–157.

Sharpe, S. (1990). Asymmetric information, bank lending and implicit contracts: A stylized model of customer relationships. *Journal of Finance*, 45(4), 1069–1087.

Shaw, E. S. (1973). *Financial Deepening in Economic Development*. Oxford: Oxford University Press.

Siamwalla, A., Pinthong, C., Poapongsakorn, N. et al. (1990). The Thai rural credit system: Public subsidies, private information, and segmented markets. *World Bank Economic Review*, 4(3), 271–295.

Siri, E. R., & Tufano, P. (1985). *The Global Financial System: A Functional Approach*. Cambridge: Harvard Business School Press.

Song, Z., Storesletten, K., & Zilibotti, F. (2011). Growing like China. *American Economic Review*, 101(1), 196–233.

Stavrakeva, V. (2020). Optimal bank regulation and fiscal capacity. *The Review of Economic Studies*, 87(2), 1034–1089.

Stein, J. C. (2002). Information production and capital allocation: Decentralized versus hierarchical firms. *The Journal of Finance*, 57(5), 1891–1921.

Stiglitz, J. E. (1990). Peer monitoring and credit markets. *World Bank Economic Review*, 4(3), 351–366.

Stockhammer, E. (2004). Financialisation and the slowdown of accumulation. *Cambridge Journal of Economics*, 28(5), 719–741.

Stulz, R. M., & Williamson, R. (2003). Culture, openness, and finance. *Journal of Financial Economics*, 70(3), 313–349.

Tadesse, S. (2002). Financial architecture and economic performance: International evidence. *Journal of Financial Intermediation*, 11(4), 429–454.

Tang, H. (2019). Peer-to-peer lenders versus banks: Substitutes or complements?. *The Review of Financial Studies*, 32(5), 1900–1938.

Thakor, A. V. (2020). Fintech and banking: What do we know?. *Journal of Financial Intermediation*, 41, 100833. https://doi.org/10.1016/j.jfi.2019.100833.

Tressel, T. (2003). Dual financial systems and inequalities in economic development. *Journal of Economic Growth*, 8(2), 223–257.

Tybout, J. R. (2000). Manufacturing firms in developing countries: How well do they do, and why? *Journal of Economic Literature*, 38(1), 11–44.

UNCTAD. (2016). The Role of Development Banks in Promoting Growth and Sustainable Development in the South (New York and Geneva: United Nations). UNCTAD/GDS/ECIDC/2016/1, https://unctad.org/en/PublicationsLibrary/gdsecidc2016d1_en.pdf.

UNIDO. (2014). UNIDO Partnership Strategy with Development Finance Institutions. Vienna: United Nations Industrial Development Organization, Strategy Paper. https://www.unido.org/sites/default/files/2014-02/UNIDO_and_financial_institutions_0.pdf.

World Bank. (2002). *World Development Report: Building Institutions for Markets*. Washington, DC.

World Bank. (2013). *Global Financial Development Report: Rethinking the Role of the State in Finance*. Washington, DC.

World Bank. (2014). *Global Financial Development Report: Financial Inclusion*. Washington, DC.

World Bank. (2015). *Global Financial Development Report 2015/2016: Long-Term Finance*. Washington, DC: The World Bank.

Xu, J. (2017). *Beyond US Hegemony in International Development*. Cambridge: Cambridge University Press.

Xu, J., & Carey, R. (2015). Post-2015 global governance of official development finance: Harnessing the renaissance of public entrepreneurship. *Journal of International Development*, 27(6), 856–880.

Xu, J., Marodon, R., Ru, X., Ren, X., & Wu, X. (2021). What are public development banks and development financing institutions? – Qualification criteria, stylized facts and development trends. *China Economic Quarterly International*, 1(4), 271–294.

Xu., J., Wang, K., & Ru, X. (2021). Funding sources of national development banks. Beijing: Institute of New Structural Economics at Peking University. New Structural Economics Development Financing Research Report No. 3.

Zingales, L. (2015). Presidential address: Does finance benefit society? *The Journal of Finance*, 70(4), 1327–1363.

Acknowledgments

We are grateful for constructive comments from the editor and anonymous reviewers. This research has been supported by the National Natural Science Foundation of China (No. 72141301, 72132010), National Social Science Fund of China (No. 2021MZD015, 21ZDA045), Natural Science Foundation of Guangdong, China (No. 2023B1515020068), Ford Foundation (No. 139355), and Special Fund of Fundamental Scientific Research Business Expense for Higher School of Central Government (No. 22wkqb04).

Cambridge Elements $\equiv$

Development Economics

Series Editor-in-Chief

Kunal Sen
UNU-WIDER and University of Manchester

Kunal Sen, UNU-WIDER Director, is Editor-in-Chief of the Cambridge Elements in Development Economics series. Professor Sen has over three decades of experience in academic and applied development economics research, and has carried out extensive work on international finance, the political economy of inclusive growth, the dynamics of poverty, social exclusion, female labour force participation, and the informal sector in developing economies. His research has focused on India, East Asia, and sub-Saharan Africa.

In addition to his work as Professor of Development Economics at the University of Manchester, Kunal has been the Joint Research Director of the Effective States and Inclusive Development (ESID) Research Centre, and a Research Fellow at the Institute for Labor Economics (IZA). He has also served in advisory roles with national governments and bilateral and multilateral development agencies, including the UK's Department for International Development, Asian Development Bank, and the International Development Research Centre.

Thematic Editors

Tony Addison
University of Copenhagen, and UNU-WIDER

Tony Addison is a Professor of Economics in the University of Copenhagen's Development Economics Research Group. He is also a Non-Resident Senior Research Fellow at UNU-WIDER, Helsinki, where he was previously the Chief Economist-Deputy Director. In addition, he is Professor of Development Studies at the University of Manchester. His research interests focus on the extractive industries, energy transition, and macroeconomic policy for development.

Chris Barret
Johnson College of Business, Cornell University

Chris Barrett is an agricultural and development economist at Cornell University. He is the Stephen B. and Janice G. Ashley Professor of Applied Economics and Management; and International Professor of Agriculture at the Charles H. Dyson School of Applied Economics and Management. He is also an elected Fellow of the American Association for the Advancement of Science, the Agricultural and Applied Economics Association, and the African Association of Agricultural Economists.

Carlos Gradín
University of Vigo

Carlos Gradín is a professor of applied economics at the University of Vigo. His main research interest is the study of inequalities, with special attention to those that exist between population groups (e.g., by race or sex). His publications have contributed to improving the empirical evidence in developing and developed countries, as well as globally, and to improving the available data and methods used.

Rachel M. Gisselquist

UNU-WIDER

Rachel M. Gisselquist is a Senior Research Fellow and member of the Senior Management Team of UNU-WIDER. She specializes in the comparative politics of developing countries, with particular attention to issues of inequality, ethnic and identity politics, foreign aid and state building, democracy and governance, and sub-Saharan African politics. Dr Gisselquist has edited a dozen collections in these areas, and her articles are published in a range of leading journals.

Shareen Joshi

Georgetown University

Shareen Joshi is an Associate Professor of International Development at Georgetown University's School of Foreign Service in the United States. Her research focuses on issues of inequality, human capital investment and grassroots collective action in South Asia. Her work has been published in the fields of development economics, population studies, environmental studies and gender studies.

Patricia Justino

UNU-WIDER and IDS – UK

Patricia Justino is a Senior Research Fellow at UNU-WIDER and Professorial Fellow at the Institute of Development Studies (IDS) (on leave). Her research focuses on the relationship between political violence, governance and development outcomes. She has published widely in the fields of development economics and political economy and is the co-founder and co-director of the Households in Conflict Network (HiCN).

Marinella Leone

University of Pavia

Marinella Leone is an assistant professor at the Department of Economics and Management, University of Pavia, Italy. She is an applied development economist. Her more recent research focuses on the study of early child development parenting programmes, on education, and gender-based violence. In previous research she investigated the short-, long-term and intergenerational impact of conflicts on health, education and domestic violence. She has published in top journals in economics and development economics.

Jukka Pirttilä

University of Helsinki, and UNU-WIDER

Jukka Pirttilä is Professor of Public Economics at the University of Helsinki and VATT Institute for Economic Research. He is also a Non-Resident Senior Research Fellow at UNU-WIDER. His research focuses on tax policy, especially for developing countries. He is a co-principal investigator at the Finnish Centre of Excellence in Tax Systems Research.

Andy Sumner

King's College London, and UNU-WIDER

Andy Sumner is Professor of International Development at King's College London; a Non-Resident Senior Fellow at UNU-WIDER and a Fellow of the Academy of Social Sciences. He has published extensively in the areas of poverty, inequality, and economic development.

About the Series

Cambridge Elements in Development Economics is led by UNU-WIDER in partnership with Cambridge University Press. The series publishes authoritative studies on important topics in the field covering both micro and macro aspects of development economics.

United Nations University World Institute for Development Economics Research

United Nations University World Institute for Development Economics Research (UNU-WIDER) provides economic analysis and policy advice aiming to promote sustainable and equitable development for all. The institute began operations in 1985 in Helsinki, Finland, as the first research centre of the United Nations University. Today, it is one of the world's leading development economics think tanks, working closely with a vast network of academic researchers and policy makers, mostly based in the Global South.

Cambridge Elements ☰

Development Economics

Elements in the Series

The 1918–20 Influenza Pandemic: A Retrospective in the Time of COVID-19
Prema-chandra Athukorala and Chaturica Athukorala

Parental Investments and Children's Human Capital in Low-to-Middle-Income Countries
Jere R. Behrman

Great Gatsby and the Global South: Intergenerational Mobility, Income Inequality, and Development
Diding Sakri, Andy Sumner and Arief Anshory Yusuf

Varieties of Structural Transformation: Patterns, Determinants, and Consequences
Kunal Sen

Economic Transformation and Income Distribution in China over Three Decades
Cai Meng, Bjorn Gustafsson and John Knight

Chilean Economic Development under Neoliberalism: Structural Transformation, High Inequality and Environmental Fragility
Andrés Solimano and Gabriela Zapata-Román

Hierarchy of Needs and the Measurement of Poverty and Standards of Living
Joseph Deutsch and Jacques Silber

New Structural Financial Economics: A Framework for Rethinking the Role of Finance in Serving the Real Economy
Justin Yifu Lin, Jiajun Xu, Zirong Yang and Yilin Zhang

A full series listing is available at: www.cambridge.org/CEDE

Milton Keynes UK
Ingram Content Group UK Ltd.
UKHW022109190224
438095UK00017B/742